LIVING ON A TIGHTROPE:
A SURVIVAL HANDBOOK
FOR PRINCIPALS

Payne, Ruby K., & Sommers, William A.
    Living on a Tightrope: a Survival Handbook for Principals.
Ruby K. Payne & Bill Sommers © 2001. 181 pp.
    Bibliography pp. 175-181.
    ISBN 0-9647437-8-7

1. Education   2. Sociology   3. Title

WILLIAM A. SOMMERS, PH.D.
RUBY K. PAYNE, PH.D.

LIVING ON A TIGHTROPE:
A SURVIVAL HANDBOOK
FOR PRINCIPALS

C*ontents*

Congratulations! You have chosen the most frustrating, satisfying, perplexing, exhilarating, fatiguing, energizing, stressful, and rewarding of careers: THE SCHOOL PRINCIPALSHIP. You will experience moments of despair, days of euphoria, times of exhilaration, and states of confusion. This book is intended to see you through the good times and the bad. Employing the knowledge and the activities contained in this handbook will maximize the likelihood of the positives outweighing the negatives.

One of the factors contributing to the dichotomy between the stresses and satisfactions of school administration is the ambiguity of rewards – there is little immediate and direct feedback to you indicating that you are effective or that you are doing a good job as principal. Furthermore, while the extensive coursework of your graduate program provided eloquent philosophical theories of administration and leadership, the practical realities were left largely for you to figure out. You often don't know if a meeting is going well, if the parents are satisfied, if your leadership strategies are appropriate, or if the students are learning. Indicators of your success are usually elusive, and the few shreds of evidence you might collect disclose little about what you should do next.

That is where this book helps. It provides a range of practical, useful, and immediately applicable strategies to know what to do when confronted with those confounding dilemmas, ambiguities, dichotomies, and enigmas that constitute the tightrope of life as a school administrator. This unique handbook provides a variety of activities to be used in the balancing act of at least three tightropes of educational management: managing relationships, managing power, and managing identity.

Managing relationships. A school principal must constantly manage relationships among individuals and groups: parents, students, community, and staff and district personnel. Attempting to stay connected with such diverse groups – each having particular interests, hidden agendas, and axes to grind while simultaneously having personal knowledge, skills, and values – provides the seedbed of many of the principal's singular frustrations.

Managing power. The role of principal may carry with it a great deal of influence. By the nature of your position you are vested with a degree of power. This power, however, provides another source of paradox. Effective managers know that their greatest strength is their capacity to empower others and that it is only when they develop leadership and decision-making power in others that they truly succeed. Therefore, the tightrope of knowing when to maintain and when to relinquish power offers another need for balance.

Managing identity. Identity is a web of relationships and is constructed with a community. It is not only how you see yourself, it's also the image others bestow upon you as a result of interactions over time. Because your identity is not fixed but rather in constant transformation, identity is a tightrope, a struggle to align yourself more congruently from within (your values, beliefs, and sense of self) and with the reciprocity of how you project yourself to the world and how others view you. It is the tightrope of authenticity – continually convincing others and ourselves that we are who and what we say we are.

The activities provided in this handbook are not intended to be prescriptions or panaceas. As you apply and adapt these strategies to your own situation, you will want to reflect on these experiences and take responsibility for your own continued learning and intellectual growth. The activities are intended to provoke an ongoing and lifelong dialogue within yourself and with others about your own high standards for your own growth and development as an authentic professional administrator.

Throughout your career, you must never lose sight of your ultimate purposes: becoming a more effective human being yourself, fostering continuous learning in students, and making our world a better place to live. The principalship is ripe with potential (and fraught with peril) in that those with whom you come in contact can leave you in a better (or worse) condition than when they came to you. You have assumed an awesome and wonderful responsibility!

- Arthur L. Costa
Kalaheo, Hawaii

Introduction

For principals to survive in the first decade of the new millennium, it is imperative that they be able to create their own tightrope. While instructional leadership has been the principal's primary role as identified in the literature, the reality is that the principal's role has become one of crisis management and an almost judicial approach to legal issues.

To further complicate the issue, no existing models adequately address the current reality. So for many principals, each day becomes a test of survival. To make it through the day somewhat unscathed is the goal.

Both Bill Sommers and I have been principals: Bill at the secondary level in an inner-city high school in Minneapolis (South High School) and I at an affluent elementary school in Barrington, Illinois (North Barrington Elementary School).

This book is an attempt to do three things: (1) provide a new mental model for the principalship that is more accurate regarding the reality; (2) articulate many of the hidden, unspoken facets of the principalship that create so many of the crises; and (3) provide tools and language to deal with the day-to-day realities of the principalship.

To guide us through the chapters, we are going to use the mental model of a tightrope and the ensuing journey across the peaks and valleys of the principalship.

- Ruby K. Payne

> *As any thinker or artist or mathematician knows, all creative endeavor has three fundamental conditions: (1) it arises from asymmetry or disorder, (2) it demands professionalism, (3) it imposes limits.*
>
> *Form and structure, selection and integration, are not playthings but necessities, and the one arena open to all is our own lives.*
>
> *- Michael Drury*

CHAPTER ONE:
ANCHOR OF STRATEGIC
ARCHITECTURE

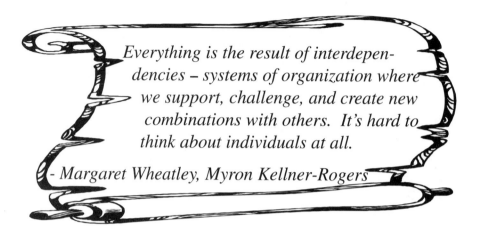

Everything is the result of interdependencies – systems of organization where we support, challenge, and create new combinations with others. It's hard to think about individuals at all.

- Margaret Wheatley, Myron Kellner-Rogers

One of the hidden structures in institutions and organizations is that of the strategic architecture. Often issues related to the strategic architecture are discussed as relationship issues. When the basic architectures are in place and they function well, fewer conflicts exist. Furthermore, when they are identified, they can be analyzed, and missing aspects or structures can be built to make the organization stronger.

Strategic architectures are those unseen, non-tangible support systems that make a big difference in the effectiveness of an institution and the level of student achievement. For example, a house has a plumbing system, a heating/cooling system, and an electrical system, all of which are hidden from view but are vital to one's ability to live in the house. Organizations have them as well. There are five strategic architectures that will be discussed here: (1) communication, (2) politics, (3) decision-making/leverage, (4) instruction, and (5) governance.

COMMUNICATION

Often communication is discussed in terms of a sender and receiver.

However, communication in organizations is much more complex.

Margaret Wheatley, in her video *Leadership and the New Science*, states

that information is so essential to the survival of an organization that

people will make up information when it isn't present. All organizations

have a **formal** and an **informal** system of communication. It weaves its

way through the fabric of the day, intermingling, confusing, and

sometimes enlightening. The formal network is the communication

received from the people who have the position and is usually in writing.

The informal network is the gossip: the networks of people, the conversa-

tions in the lounge, parking lot, and hall. A general rule of thumb exists:

<u>The more closed and guarded the formal network, the greater the reliance</u>

<u>on the informal network</u>.

To analyze the communication architecture you rely upon, this next

activity is recommended.

ACTIVITY 1.1

In this table, check where you get your best information. For example, for information about your school board, does your best information (accurate and timely) come from memos, official meetings, a professional relationship, community members?

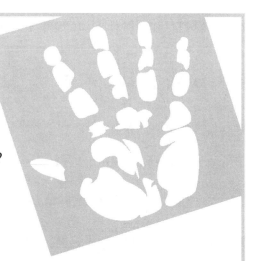

	Memos	Official Meetings	Relationships	Community Gossip
Board				
Superintendent				
Principal				
Parents				
Students				
Teachers				
Secretaries				
Custodians				
Food service				
Aides, assistants, other support staff				

ACTIVITY 1.2

In your current situation, does your best information (accurate and timely) come from the formal network or the informal network? In the grid from 1.1, put parentheses around the sources whose information is often partly inaccurate.

To be effective, a principal needs to listen to both types of sources. A process to follow is:

1. Read the formal.
2. Verify the informal.
3. Verify the source of the information.
4. Verify the network of the informal source.

REMEMBER: IN SCHOOL DISTRICTS, SECRETARIES AND CUSTODIANS ARE TWO OF THE TOP SOURCES OF INFORMAL INFORMATION. THEY SEE ALL THE MEMOS IN THE TRASH AND OVERHEAR THE CONVERSATIONS. THEY ALSO OVERHEAR ONES YOU DON'T.

ACTIVITY 1.3

From the grid in 1.1, identify your five best sources of information.

ACTIVITY 1.4

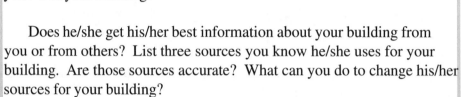

What is the
communication
architecture that your
superintendent uses for
you? For your building?

   Does he/she get his/her best information about your building from
you or from others? List three sources you know he/she uses for your
building. Are those sources accurate? What can you do to change his/her
sources for your building?

ACTIVITY 1.5

What roles do your
custodian, secretary, and
support staff play in the
formal and informal communication structure in your building?

ACTIVITY 1.6

How can you build a
better strategic
architecture of communication?

POLITICS

To understand political infrastructures, two concepts need to be discussed: (1) triangulation and (2) the tribe versus the individual. Political architectures resemble a jellyfish or an octopus. The body represents the tribe; the legs or tentacles represent the individuals. Just as it's difficult to see the legs or the tentacles all at once, so is it difficult to see the long links of political architectures.

The tribe or body of the jellyfish represents the accepted way of doing things. The tentacles or individuals represent the links to people or thinking outside the tribe.

REMEMBER: POLITICAL ARCHITECTURES OPERATE WITH NO REGARD TO INSTITUTIONAL BOUNDARIES. THEY ONLY HAVE POWER WITHIN YOUR BUILDING TO THE EXTENT THAT THEY ARE LINKED AND TENTACLED TO THE LARGER COMMUNITY. IF ONE KNOWS WHERE THE TENTACLES ARE, THE LESS ONE IS STUNG.

Triangulation

Triangulation is the pattern in which two people or groups will side with or against another individual or group. The less stable a situation politically or the more scarce the resources, the greater the amount of triangulation. In politically charged situations, which individuals or groups will side with each other changes.

Triangulation limits the effectiveness of the system's architecture. This concept also has been identified in families, small departments, and large organizations. The basic structure is that person "A" is mad or hurt by person "B." Instead of talking to person "B" to clear up the issue between them, person "A" talks to person "C" about the issue. Sometimes person "A" wants empathy and understanding. Sometimes, however, person "A" is intent upon a power play to coerce or sabotage Person "B" into compliance. In either case, person "C" tells person "B" what person "A" wants or gives information that isn't particularly helpful. This triangulation causes other people to be involved, which widens the issue from two people to more and more participants. If this triangulation is not addressed, organizations start choosing sides, thereby draining energy from the system and diverting focus from the organizational mission.

When designing system architecture that promotes authentic dialogue among individuals, departments, and the organization, the principal must be vigilant in confronting triangulation when it's noticed. Left unattended, triangulation usually increases and results in destructive relationships, inaccurate information, and unproductive relationships that reduce effectiveness and efficiency. In Chapter Three we'll discuss cognitive and affective conflict. Triangulation occurs with both.

ACTIVITY 1.7

1. Identify triangulation patterns in your organization.
2. Has this pattern been going on for a long time, or is it a recent development?
3. What is the outcome of the triangulation pattern?
4. How can you stop triangulation and develop authentic dialogue?
5. What recommendations do you have about structural architecture that will decrease triangulation?

ACTIVITY 1.8

To find out who heads the tribe(s) in your attendance area and district, the following process can be used:

Use this visual to map it out. First, put the name(s) of the individuals who have the most influence. Then highlight those you have a positive relationship with. Influence is defined as those individuals who have the ability to change opinions.

Your Political Arena of Influence and Access

Parents ◯ ◯ ◯ ◯

Board members ◯ ◯ ◯ ◯ ◯ ◯ ◯

Superintendent ◯ ◯ ◯ ◯

Central office ◯ ◯ ◯ ◯

Principals ◯ ◯ ◯ ◯

Teachers ◯ ◯ ◯ ◯

Other ◯ ◯ ◯ ◯

ACTIVITY 1.9

To begin identifying the tentacles, use ocular analysis (eyeballing and observation) to find the individuals with power. Look at the following indicators: (a) money, (b) longstanding community relationships, (c) outspoken maverick with guts, (d) access to elected decision-makers, and (e) gatekeepers. For each category, identify people by name. Indicate whether they are a member of the tribe or an individual outside the tribe.

Money	Long-standing Community Relationships	Outspoken Maverick with Guts	Access to Elected Decision-makers	Gatekeepers

Once you know who runs the tribe and who the individuals are who interact on the fringes, you can better calculate triangulation.

ACTIVITY 1.10

Draw an octopus or a
jellyfish. For your building only,
write the names of the individuals who
represent the tribe. On the tentacles, write the names of the individuals
who affect the politics of the building by taking positions. On which
issues are they with the tribe? On which issues are they outside the tribe?

ACTIVITY 1.11

Who in your ACTIVITY 1.10 has
the longest tentacles, i.e., the longest
links to the community? Whom do these tentacles touch?

ACTIVITY 1.12

Repeat ACTIVITY 1.10 for
your district.

DECISION-MAKING/LEVERAGE

Peter Block (1987) created the matrix on the next page in order to
assess whom in your organization agrees with your vision for the future
and whom you trust. Identifying these two dimensions, agreement and
trust, will allow you to develop different approaches to people in different
categories.

DECISION-MAKING MATRIX

High

BEDFELLOWS (fence-sitters)	ALLIES
ADVERSARIES	OPPONENTS

Agreement (along left, vertical axis)

Low   High

Trust

Allies – high trust/high agreement
Opponents – high trust/low agreement
Bedfellows – low trust/high agreement
Fence-sitters – low trust/unknown agreement
Adversaries – low trust/low agreement

Allies and opponents are trustworthy individuals. Allies don't need a lot of maintenance. They are the people who are already working hard with you, and you value their support. A saying from the business world applies here: "Once you've made the sale, shut up!" However, you do need to maintain the relationships.

Opponents can be your best friends. They trust you enough to say, "You are wrong." They may not agree with you, but there is a high level of trust. With high trust, you know you can be honest and get valuable feedback without feeling you'll be sabotaged; the points they make should be taken seriously. They will tell you when they think you're wrong but will remain your friend and will discuss issues above the table. Make sure you listen to your opponents. They can help identify cautions to think through prior to a firm decision.

People in categories of low trust are a concern. The bedfellows will be politically valuable when enlisting support for a particular project, for reaching goals, or for resolving issues. Because of low trust, however, the principal needs to be aware that other motives may drive their support. Fence-sitters provide opportunity to attract people to your vision for what you want to accomplish. Members of this group may warrant some of your time because they could provide more support for your projects. But because of low trust, keep your eyes open.

The last category – adversaries – doesn't deserve much time or energy. This group doesn't trust you (and vice versa), and there is little agreement on issues. Principals sometimes spend too much time and energy trying to convince adversaries to support their issues. I think this simply isn't worth the time or effort. If the majority of the system is in this category, then you may want to revisit your ideas. Normally 10% or fewer are in this category. Stay cordial, but spend very little time trying to convince. Your time is better spent with fence-sitters and opponents. The opponents will help you strategize the substantive issues that need to be addressed. Remember, there is trust with opponents, just not agreement on the issue. If you are to be successful, you will have to answer the questions that opponents will ask. This makes you either rethink your goals and approach, or it will make you stronger in your advancement of the project.

A caution: People may be in different categories on different issues. Don't pigeonhole people from one issue to all issues. There may be individuals who seem to be always adversarial, but keep in mind that people have different viewpoints on issues. It would be a mistake to generalize, based on one issue.

Using Block's template (see p. 23) may help you plan and implement your next initiative.

ACTIVITY 1.13

1. With whom do you spend most of your time? Why?
2. What is your current strategy for dealing with opponents, adversaries, et al.?
3. What seems to be working or not working?
4. How can you change your approach by using this template?
5. Read Chapter Five of *The Empowered Manager* (Block, 1987) for alternative strategies.

REMEMBER THAT DECISIONS OFTEN ARE MADE ON THE BASIS OF FEELINGS AND RELATIONSHIPS. IN FACT, FEELINGS ARE A FORM OF DATA. NEVER UNDERESTIMATE THE IMPACT OF EMOTIONS ON DECISIONS.

Process

Here is a process that can be used to make decisions:

1. Gather key individuals (those with influence and whom the decision most affects).
2. Identify the greater good.
3. Give everyone the pertinent data.
4. Identify whom they need to share data with.
5. Identify a "thinking time," a time for people to think about the issues before the committee convenes for discussion.
6. Get a short (two to three sentences) written response from each person. Prepare copies for all.
7. Respond to written comments. Formulate a plan.

SCULPTING THE ORGANIZATION
FROM A THIRD-PARTY PERSPECTIVE

*I don't know who discovered the ocean,
but I know it wasn't the fish.*

- Marshall McLuhan

Occasionally we become so enmeshed in our day-to-day operations

that it's hard to maintain overall perspective regarding the system. When

this happens it may be useful to try to move toward a third-party

perspective.

ACTIVITY 1.14

Map the educational system
in your organization:

This activity can be done for
the district, a school, a committee,
etc. It should help you as principal
gain a new point of view. You'll
need a large piece of paper (butcher-
block paper on the wall could be used,
too), colored pencils or markers, and
masking tape.

First, develop some symbols like a
picture of buildings to identify different sites,
walls for barriers, and people for stakeholders or community groups, etc.
When you have most of the elements identified, either draw them or
place them on the paper far apart if the relationships are estranged or near
if the relationships are close. These can be drawn or taped onto the paper.

Second, draw relationships. You might use highways or railroad
tracks for wide-open communication; straight or crooked, depending on
how direct or indirect; dotted lines for under construction; and rocks or
walls for barriers.

Third, use green for growing and thriving connections, yellow where
the system is static or in a holding pattern or caution is called for, and red
where the system is not in a healthy state.

Fourth, once you have a picture of the existing system, stand back and
look for omissions. Sometimes the macro view of a system helps identify
errors.

Fifth, where would you build a new road, a bridge, and new relationship? Where would you remove barriers to enhance communication?
Where would it be advantageous for both parties or groups to repair or
replace a connection?

Turn the picture or stand to view the system from other perspectives.
Answer the previous questions from a new perspective.

INSTRUCTION

A systematic infrastructure to monitor learning and enhance instruction is needed. There are five pieces that must be in place in some manner in order to consistently and systematically monitor learning. (See the Appendix for an in-depth article and examples.)

These five pieces are:

1. Identifying individual students by quartile and subgroup.
2. Identifying the amount of time by subject, by grade level (elementary) or by course (secondary) that is given to content pieces and skill pieces.
3. Identifying measures of growth against standards.
4. Identifying buildingwide interventions for those students who don't make the necessary growth AT THE TIME THEY'RE NOT MAKING THE GROWTH.
5. Embedding the four pieces above into the daily life of the school through the campus plan AND the weekly memo.

GOVERNANCE

Sometimes the picture is clouded even further by the external governing structures that can be seen. Legally for schools, the governing group is usually the district school board. With the advent of site-based decision-making, however, yet another structure is in the picture.

Some site councils have been very effective and are able to act as a conduit for information and feedback. But many site councils are having problems being caught between an advisory role and decision-making. I suggest that site councils cannot be decision-makers. In the end the person who will be held accountable for the school is the principal. Obviously the more input and commitment a principal and the administrative team can get, the better off they are.

Many times the principal and the administrative team get caught between conflicting desires while trying to balance that conflict with research and policies. Neither the principal nor the site council in most schools I know controls the staffing budget or allocations. Without control over these two elements, how do a principal and site council effectively make a difference? All too often it involves rearranging the deck chairs of the Titanic.

Schools all over the United States have multiple communities to deal with under the auspices of one school. One problem is getting representation from all segments. When one or two vocal ideologies shows up at meetings and proposes solutions, the principal normally must try to represent the whole school environment. This can set up conflicts within the school community that may delay decisions, stop actions to solve problems, and create adversarial

© aha! Process, Inc. • 1-800-424-9484

relationships in the community that are exactly the opposite of the intended outcome.

Another issue that arises in site councils is the confusion of leadership and management. For the leadership of a school to have ideas, information, and involvement from parents and community can be very effective. By acquiring and reviewing the data, which are the results of the school program, site councils can helpfully recommend new policies, goals, and objectives. But if the site council spends time micromanaging the principal, administering rules and regulations, and attempting to operate the school, the roles and responsibilities get cloudy. Staff, students, and community get confused as to who is in charge of the school operation. There are charter schools that are operated by a board and may be working well, but this issue must be clarified.

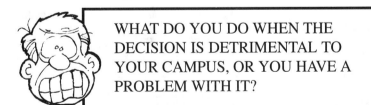

WHAT DO YOU DO WHEN THE DECISION IS DETRIMENTAL TO YOUR CAMPUS, OR YOU HAVE A PROBLEM WITH IT?

To <u>impact</u> the planning and decision-making in your district:

1. Provide data (either for or against) <u>in writing</u>.

2. Circulate the written data. Why? For honesty, for greater influence, to help people (including staff people in your school) know where you stand, to build trust.

ACTIVITY 1.15

Finish the story:

Once upon a time, a principal got a memo from central office informing him/her that his/her building must _____.
The teachers union stated that it supported the decision. In your teachers lounge, the teachers are saying _____. Your informal source in central office says _____. You know that in your building if _____ opposes it, no one will speak for it. You also know that if _____ speaks for it, it also will happen. And you know that in your building if _____ doesn't agree, he/she will go to _____ to get it changed. Further, you know that _____ is a very good friend of one of the members of the school board. Tomorrow your site-based council is going to make a decision. You as principal do/do not support the memo. You know you can influence the decision by talking to ____ _____. You also know you can influence the decision through procedure, so you _____. Because this decision will greatly influence instruction, you _____.
In the end, _____.

CHAPTER TWO:
SAFETY NET OF RELATIONSHIPS

If love is creative stuff,
it is for that very reason not a continuous state,
anymore than genius works at gale force every hour.
All creative energy has winters and summers,
planting and harvest,
with time between for growth.
Love wears a thousand masks …
at times …
it is like a light breath,
at times,
like a wrestling bout.

- Michael Drury

Where are you going?
Who will go with you?
These are two questions
everyone must ask. You will
get in trouble if you get them
out of order.

- Sam Keen

Relationships are the safety net that allows a leader to walk the

tightrope, fall, and still be safe. Relationships provide comfort, strength,

assistance, and the assurance that there are people to help.

RELATIONSHIPS YOU RELY UPON

ACTIVITY 2.1

Who are your key relationships?
Map them out.

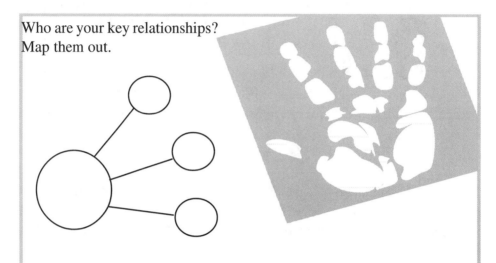

1. Put your name in the middle circle.
2. Make circles to indicate three key relationships you have in your building.
3. Make more circles to indicate three key relationships you have in the district.
4. Make more circles to indicate three key relationships you have in the community.
5. Draw a square for the people to whom you answer. If it's a positive relationship, draw a straight line. If it isn't a positive relationship, draw a broken line.
6. Draw in three triangles for people you would like to develop a relationship with that would make you more effective.

RELATIONSHIPS ABOVE YOU

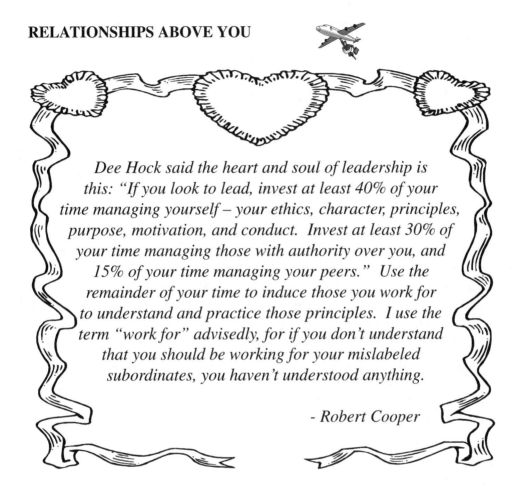

Dee Hock said the heart and soul of leadership is this: "If you look to lead, invest at least 40% of your time managing yourself – your ethics, character, principles, purpose, motivation, and conduct. Invest at least 30% of your time managing those with authority over you, and 15% of your time managing your peers." Use the remainder of your time to induce those you work for to understand and practice those principles. I use the term "work for" advisedly, for if you don't understand that you should be working for your mislabeled subordinates, you haven't understood anything.

- Robert Cooper

ACTIVITY 2.2

What are your key relationships with the people above you? Map them out.

What activities do you do to manage those relationships? Some recommended activities are:

a. Make certain your superintendent has no surprises. Make sure he/she hears about it from you first.

b. Go to the superintendent in the summer. Identify your campus goals and personnel issues for the next year and say, "Here is what I would like to do next year. How much heat can you take for me?" It's vital to understand that a superintendent can only deal with so many issues. Let him/her decide what he/she can handle with the board.

c. Identify any issues in the building that will create parent flak and board noise. Ask him/her if he/she has a preference about how you deal with them.

d. Ask him/her if there are things that can occur in your building to strengthen his/her position with the board or help the board members meet their goals.

e. Cultivate a good relationship with the superintendent's secretary and the board secretary (sometimes the same person). Make certain that if there is an emergency the information you provided will be heard even if you cannot make contact with the superintendent.

f. Cover the chain-of-command issues by always addressing your supervisor but cc-ing copies to the superintendent or whomever makes key decisions on your behalf.

g. If you receive a call from a board member or talk to one, make sure you apprise the superintendent of that conversation (before it occurs, if possible.)

h. Each week a couple of days before the superintendent sends out the weekly update to board members, send him/her a memo and attach items of interest, awards, etc., that have occurred recently in your building.

i. Send an FYI memo.

j. Send a "Here's an idea you had that I initiated" memo.

k. Think: How do I make him/her look good?

MANAGING TIME FOR RELATIONSHIPS

Time is the principal's most valuable commodity. Time also signals

for the staff what the principal deems important. I have used the

metaphor of a cat wearing a bell around its neck. The principal is

observed all day, every day. Like parents with their children, where

the principal spends his/her time signals importance. Stephen Covey

has written many books on leadership. One of his ideas is about

where you spend your time. The matrix on the next page has axes of

important and urgent.

TIME-MANAGEMENT MATRIX

	Urgent	Not Urgent
Important	**QUADRANT I** • Crises • Pressing problems • Deadline-driven projects, meeting preparation	**QUADRANT II** • Preparation • Prevention • Values clarification • Planning • Relationship-building • True re-creation • Empowerment
Not Important	**QUADRANT III** • Interruptions, some phone calls • Some mail, some reports • Some meetings • Many proximate, pressing matters • Many popular activities	**QUADRANT IV** • Trivia, busywork • Junk mail • Some phone calls • Time-wasters • "Escape" activities

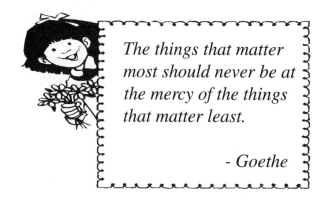

The things that matter most should never be at the mercy of the things that matter least.

- Goethe

ACTIVITY 2.3

1. Track your daily calendar.
   What percentage of time are you
   spending in each quadrant?
2. As you look ahead at your calendar, what percentage
   of planned time is in each quadrant?
3. What support systems need to be in place in order to
   spend more time in Quadrant II?

MAKING AND BREAKING RELATIONSHIPS

Deposits	Withdrawals
Seek first to understand	Seek first to be understood
Keeping promises	Breaking promises
Kindnesses, courtesies	Unkindnesses, discourtesies
Clarifying expectations	Violating expectations
Loyalty to the absent	Disloyalty, duplicity
Apologies	Pride, conceit, arrogance
Open to feedback	Rejecting feedback

Chart taken from *The Seven Habits of Highly Effective People* (1989)

It is important to be aware of our deposits and withdrawals. If we are not conscious of our emotional balance sheet, we might be out of resources and not know it. As you look at the chart above, use it to answer the two-part question in ACTIVITY 2.4.

ACTIVITY 2.4

Under what circumstances
have you made deposits – and withdrawals?

IT IS IMPORTANT TO NOTE THAT
SOME RELATIONSHIPS COMPROMISE
PERSONAL INTEGRITY. IS THIS A
RELATIONSHIP YOU WANT?

ACTIVITY 2.5

Do you have any relationships
that compromise personal integrity?
If so, how can you deal with this
situation?

Several years ago my son asked me, "Dad, what do you do all day?"

That question has caused a lot of thought over the years. I responded by

saying, "I go to meetings and manage conflicts." As I think about my day

as principal, that is mainly what I do. One of the most time-consuming

demands is managing conflict. We tend to think of conflict as bad.

Conflict, however, is not inherently bad.

When you have people with diversity of thought, gender, ethnicity,

socioeconomic status, etc., there will be conflict. Bob Chadwick (1997), a nationally known speaker on consensus-building, says conflict is a result of five things: change, power, scarcity, diversity, and civility. I agree that those five account for most of our difficulty. What conflicts are you dealing with in these areas? There is a type of conflict, though, that can be healthy for an organization.

In an article by Amason, et al. (1995), a type of conflict is identified that can actually enhance the health of an organization. "C"-type conflict is cognitive in nature and focuses on substantive issues related to differences of opinion. This type of conflict involves the assumptions that underlie a particular stance, and the support system provides the safety net to discuss these issues out in the open. Having a forum for this kind of conflict has been shown to improve team effectiveness and produce better decisions, along with increased commitment, cohesiveness, empathy, and understanding.

"A"-type conflict, on the other hand, lowers team effectiveness by fostering hostility, distrust, cynicism, and avoidance. This type of conflict focuses on personalized anger or resentment directed mainly at specific individuals rather than ideas. It tends to be more emotionally charged. The results of "A" conflict are destructive, leading to poorer decisions, as well as decreased commitment, cohesiveness, and empathy.

Generally, healthier organizations tend to be characterized by
(1) discussions of core issues, not trivial points; (2) creativity, not short-
term expediency; (3) broad participation in discussion, not domination by
a few vocal people; and (4) the integration of diverse perspectives, not the
threat of anger, resentment, or retribution.

Does your school or school system encourage the expression of "C"
conflict? Or does it get bogged down in "A" conflict?

RELATIONSHIPS THAT ARE ADVERSARIAL AND INVOLVE CONFLICT

ACTIVITY 2.6

Map the relationships that you have in your building that are adversarial and involve conflict with others in your building.

Map those relationships you have in the district that are adversarial.

ACTIVITY 2.7

Look at your
adversarial relationships.
What would it take to move
from "A" to "C"?

    If it's just a personality conflict, what can you do to make the
relationship better? If it's one that compromises integrity, what can you
do to maintain communication but not compromise your integrity?

Group Conflicts in Your Building

ACTIVITY 2.8

Map out these conflicts.

Conflicts in Your Building Between and Among Individual Staff Members

ACTIVITY 2.9

Map out these conflicts.

ACTIVITY 2.10

In the next chapter, very specific strategies will be given to address the conflicts. *Continue the story of the principal. Who are the other characters that will go into the story?*

    Once upon a time, a principal went home with a migraine headache. _____ was mad at _____. Not only that, _____ got _____ and _____ on his/her side. He/she got _____ and _____ on his/her side. Then one of the teachers named _____ went to her classroom upset and told the students a few things about the situation. Then _____ called his/her favorite parent named _____ to get support. In the teachers lounge, _____ was going on. You have been in a principals meeting all morning and, as you're leaving to go back to your building, your friend in the central office stops you and says, _____. It's time for lunch, and you think about _____. When you return, your secretary follows you into your office and says, _____. So the principal _____.

    There is a Zen story about groups of people. A person traveled with a Zen master to look in on a group of people. When they approached this group, everyone was complaining, blaming others, and crying. They were all sitting around a big kettle of stew. Each person had a spoon. However, the spoon was too long from the handle to the ladle so the people could not get the ladle to their own mouth. The handle was too hot to move their hand closer to make the distance shorter. The Zen master said that this was an example of hell.

The Zen master then took the person to another group of people. It was the same setting as before with a kettle of stew in the middle of the group with spoon handles too long, but these people were smiling, laughing, and seemed very happy with their situation. The person looked around and found that each member of the group was feeding someone else with his/her spoon. The Zen master said that this was heaven.

CHAPTER THREE:
WINDS OF BELIEF SYSTEMS AND CHANGE

Probably the winds that knock the most principals off their tightrope are the (1) winds of change, (2) winds of belief systems, (3) conflicts between governing structures, and (4) organizational cycles. Often there are crosswinds, downdrafts, updrafts, headwinds, and tailwinds.

When a principal can identify the source of the wind or the cause of the wind, it becomes much easier to identify the available options.

WINDS OF BELIEF SYSTEMS

Two of the best pieces of work on belief systems are by Mark Gerzon and Elliott Eisner. Here is a chart with a compilation of their work.

BELIEFS AND THEIR IMPLICATIONS

Belief	Purpose of Education	Vocabulary	Method of Evaluation	Common Comments
Cognitive processors	To teach students to think	Thinking skills, intellectual development, problem-solving	Observation of performance	"As long as they can think, it doesn't matter what we teach ..."
Self-actualizers	To allow students to develop as individuals to their level of potential	Peak experience, whole child, affective, nurturance	IEP (Individualized Education Plan), holistic, developmental progression of skills	"I just want her to feel good about herself. I am not going to push her; it could harm her ..."
Technologists	To have students meet set of standards and demonstrate their learning against those standards	Measurable learning, task analysis, input, output, diagnosis of systems, computers, distance learning	Pre and post tests, gain scores, growth against standardized measures	"Is he learning or not? Did he make any growth? I don't care how he feels about it ..."

Belief	Purpose of Education	Vocabulary	Method of Evaluation	Common Comments
Academic rationalists	To learn a discipline and be able to use that discipline	Classics; humanities; traditional curriculum; rigor; basics; scholarly, conceptual themes	Mastery of content, achievement testing, summative testing	"My job is to teach the content; his job is to learn it ..."
Social reconstruc-tionists	To nurture social conscience and look out for well-being of world now and in future	Survival, consumer education, environment, peace education	Service hours; involvement in social reconstruction activities, editorials	"What does it matter what they know if there is no longer a world to live in?"
Moral standard bearers	To build character and moral human beings who can participate in immoral society	Character education, moral imperatives, God and country, vouchers, charter schools, privacy	Essays, knowledge of basics and classics tested	"There is so much evil in the world. They need to learn to obey. There is no point in learning anything but the basics and the classics."
Brain-based-learning devotees	To interact with language and environment to make meaning	Brain-based connections, making meaning, thematic curriculum, patterns	Rubrics, projects, performance assessments, identification of patterns	"If students cannot make meaning and identify patterns, why bother? Little else is remembered."

ACTIVITY 3.1

1. What are the primary beliefs in your building?
2. In the last arguments among the staff, which beliefs surfaced?
3. What is the primary belief in the prevailing political influences?

In addition, further winds come from organizational cycles.

CYCLES IN ORGANIZATIONS

Most organizations progress through a predictable evolution. The

description on the next page is adapted from a book called *Barbarians to*

Bureaucrats (1989) by Lawrence Miller.

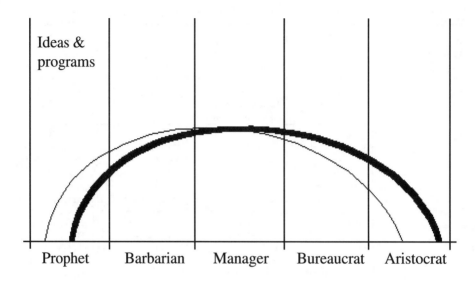

New way – thin line
Results – bold line

A staff member or small group of staff members gets an idea to solve

a problem, increase achievement, or make the organization more

productive. These persons take on the role of a prophet: They have

vision, they have a plan, and they have the ability to attract others to that

vision. There is growing interest in and commitment to the idea. Others in

the organization don't believe this new program will work, or they take a

wait-and-see attitude. As people start doing things differently, a little

positive change is taking place, but that is dismissed as the Hawthorne

Effect – "just lucky" or some other external reason.

The second stage begins with a barbarian. Sometimes this is the same

person as the prophet, but this person believes so strongly in the new

idea or program that he/she is willing to take on the establish-

ment, recruit people to the cause, and receive additional support

from others in the organization. This is a powerful position

because barbarians walk their talk, make tremendous sacrifices,

and are totally immersed in a new way of doing things. The results start to

show that the new idea is working, so more attention is paid to the pro-

gram and the barbarian.

In the manager phase, the barbarian(s) sense intuitively that they have

gone as far as they can with this idea and start looking for another plan,

another cause, or just some rest since the energy drain has been very high.

Remember, it takes 90% of the fuel to get a spacecraft into orbit. A

manager takes over and says, in effect, "Let's keep doing what we've been

doing because it's working. Look at the results." The early efforts are

still showing positive gains. The barbarians have probably dropped out.

"Same ol', same ol'" is not what excites or attracts prophets and

barbarians. Land and Jarman, in their book *Break-Point and Beyond*

(1992), say this is a bifurcation point. If left unchanged, a natural drop-off in results and productivity will occur naturally. An organization should start looking for the next step to keep moving in a positive direction, but managers usually win, and the status quo takes over. It's hard for those in charge to change when productivity is high.

The next stage is where bureaucrats assume control. Their main job is to say, "No, let's not change anything." Prophets and barbarians have left for other areas or sit on the sidelines. Managers are starting to see the decline in human energy. In the final stages of atrophy, the complacent aristocracy assumes command, resulting in an increasingly pronounced drop in productivity itself. Unfortunately, the energy drain has caused the system to sag, and the creative adapters (who make up the prophets and barbarians) usually have left for other organizations or have isolated into their own area.

As results, productivity, and more importantly the human potential have dropped off, leaders at the top of the organization are now taking heat from their constituency – like Board of Education members, parents, and community. They often take the "DAD" approach: Decide, Announce, and Defend. They start putting money into individual projects to ease the pressure and begin building a group of "yes" people who will protect them.

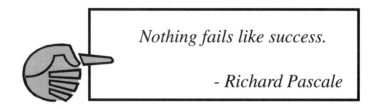

Nothing fails like success.

- Richard Pascale

Without unfiltered feedback, not much creative production will happen until a major upheaval takes place. Then the whole process starts over again. Unfortunately, all this takes time, money, and most of the vital human energy out of the system.

LAND AND JARMAN

In *Break-Point and Beyond* Land and Jarman discuss three qualities needed for organizations to cope with change.

The first requirement is the need for creativity. There are usually unrealized talents and potentials in organizations that may not be included in current leadership models. This requires a shift from logical, linear thinking to innovative and discontinuous thinking. Basically there's a need to change from doing things differently to doing different things.

A second need is connectivity. How we develop partnerships between people and among ideas is essential in solving changing issues and dilemmas before us. We're all interdependent, whether we want to be or not. It will take the combined connections of all elements of the organ-

ization to thrive in the future.

The third concept is future pull. Not only do we need to be creative

and connect parts, we need to think about the desired future, develop a

clear vision, and help pull the organization in the right direction.

Principals need to make day-to-day connections to the future and provide

the relevance of the school's plan to that future.

ACTIVITY 3.2

1. Are you finding ways to use
    your and your staff's creativity?
2. Are you finding ways to connect
    staff members, programs, community, etc.?
3. What are the trends that will pull you and/or your organization into the
    future?

BECKHARD'S CHANGE MODEL

Richard Beckhard in *Organizational Transitions* (1987) devised the

following formula to describe change in organizations: $C = D \times V \times F > R$.

"C" stands for the change you want in yourself or the organization.

"D" is the dissatisfaction with the current situation. You may want to

rate this on a scale of 1 to 10 or discuss how deeply people feel the

dissatisfaction.

"V" is the vision for the future or the preferred situation. This must be described in detail in order for staff to know where the organization and its people want to go.

"F" stands for the first steps toward the new vision. Can you and/or members of the organization write down action steps on how you will get to the preferred future?

"R" is the resistance to any change. How strong will resistance be?

When the combination of "D," "V," and "F" is greater than "R," then the system will move toward the future vision.

When you assess your organization ...

ACTIVITY 3.3

1. Which elements of the formula are strongest/weakest?
2. If you begin the change today, what predictions for success do you make?
3. How can you improve the chances of success?

POLITICAL STORMS

The following story demonstrates a process that can help reduce the fury of political storms. I learned this process from Bob Chadwick (1997), who trains many people in consensus-building processes.

HOCKEY STORY

Our high school's athletic director came into my office and said some

parents wanted to talk to her about the hockey situation. She wanted

me as principal to attend. First, I didn't know there was a hockey situation

and second, hockey in Minnesota is like football in Texas. We decided on

a date and time. Of course, even though I come to work at 6:00 a.m.

("zero hour" starts at 6:20 a.m.), the parents wanted to meet at 6:00 that

evening. I thought a few parents, the athletic director, and I would meet to

discuss the issues.

At 6:00 p.m. five parents, the athletic director, and the head coach

showed up at my office. It was my first year as principal in this building,

and I had not personally met the young hockey coach, so he didn't know

me either. By 6:05 another five parents and the assistant hockey coach

arrived. I moved the group to a conference room to accommodate

everyone. By 6:15 we had 25 parents, three hockey coaches, the athletic

director, and myself in a classroom, and there was a lot of buzzing. Not

knowing what to expect, I sat listening to individuals with a variety of

concerns. By 6:30 there were more than 40 people in the room, and it

appeared no one had a process for discussing the issues as a group. After consulting with the AD, I used a process I had learned from Bob

Chadwick.

I asked the parents a general question: "Does anyone want to share

their concerns with the larger group?" By 7:00 several parents had

brought up their issues while the coaches, the AD, and I listened. I again

asked if any parents had other issues they wanted to put out for discussion.

By 7:15 the parents had finished. At that point I asked John, the head

hockey coach, what issues he thought needed to be addressed and how he

felt about the situation. As John started to talk, some parents tried to

interrupt with additional comments. I stopped them and said we

had been respectfully listening to them for an hour, and now it was John's

turn to speak. There were a few "looks," but the room got quiet. John

proceeded to explain issues he thought were relevant and how he felt

about the season that had just started. When he was done, I stayed focused

on John and asked, "What would be the worst possible outcome of this

meeting for you?" John thought for a minute, then said that if he resigned,

if the parents wouldn't support the program, and if our team didn't win the

city championship. I was watching the non-verbals of the parents while

John talked. I could tell that John had hit the mark by the way the parents were responding. When John finished, I returned to the parents.

I asked the parents what was the worst possible outcome they could imagine out of this meeting. The first parent who spoke said that if John resigned, that would be the worst. In my mind I knew the meeting had turned because I had gotten agreement on the worst possible scenario. Once you get agreement on anything, usually you can get the sides to agree on other issues. Several other parents spoke and said similar things John had already covered, with a few minor additions. I stayed with the parents. My question to them was, "What are the best possible outcomes that could result from this meeting?"

Parents indicated that they would like John to form a parent liaison position, work with the booster groups, and talk more to the players when they get demoted so they understand what the issues were. I then went back to John and asked what were the best possible outcomes for the hockey program. He identified similar ideas and added a few more from a historical perspective. (John had played on this team several years ago as a student.)

After John and the other coaches had finished speaking, I asked John, "What actions are you willing to take in order to foster the best possible outcomes you have just mentioned?" John and the coaches

described what plans they had, what they would be willing to do, and the

help they needed. Then, back to the parents, I asked them the same

question about what actions they were willing to take. There was a match

on about three points. It was now 9:00. I said, as I understood it, John

will do 1, 2, 3, and the parents will do 1, 2, 3. I then said I had been at the

school for 15 hours straight, and I was going home. When I left, the

coaches and the parents were still talking about how they were going to

work together.

I'm sure that some issues weren't resolved and that some parents

weren't happy with some parts of the process, but I didn't get a single

call from another parent the rest of that season or the next. The AD

wanted to know how to use that process for conflict management, and

John called me later to thank me for my role in the meeting.

It's paramount that leaders in organizations have cognitive

maps to help keep them on the road toward their goals. NASA

reports the spaceships are off course more than 80% of the time

when going to the moon, but they do eventually hit their target. The

challenge is being able to make mid-course corrections while keeping your eye on the goal.

As schools and districts get more and more complex, with more and more people wanting their issues addressed, it becomes increasingly vital for leaders to know where the goal is, the nature of the signals telling them that their direction is correct, and how to know if they're straying from the goal.

LEADERSHIP CHANGES

What do you do when the leadership above you changes, specifically the superintendent?

If you're aware of the political infrastructures, you can know why some of it is happening.

Three of the reasons superintendents lose their job are a decrease in funding, redistricting, and curriculum changes. In addition, a few superintendents lose their job because of inappropriate sexual activities or financial irregularities.

Sometimes there is a board election. Members were elected primarily to get rid of a superintendent, coach, et al.

How does a superintendent go about getting another job? Why does that affect you as a principal?

Some superintendents belong to a "stable," which is the verbiage used among superintendent search firms. There are privately held superintendent search firms, as well as public associations. In almost every state, the school-board association of that state will do superintendent searches for districts. But in the privately owned search firms, the firm does the search – i.e., it screens the candidates. Often the "paper cut" is done before the position is ever advertised. The "paper cut" comprises the applications the board will see. Often the search firm will narrow it down to 10 applications. As part of the search, the search team identifies, through interviewing and looking at documents, the primary attributes the board is looking for in its candidates.

If a superintendent who is part of a stable gets in trouble (difficult board, controversial issues, etc.), the search firm will make him/her a part of the paper cut of other openings, particularly if the superintendent meets several of the primary criteria. Sometimes, to maintain the reputation of the search firm, it will ask superintendents to apply so that the firm can have a good slate for the board.

The "stable" then becomes a sort of insurance for both the

superintendent and the firm.

If your superintendent is part of a "stable," some of the decisions

made may be more understandable.

ACTIVITY 3.4

How do leadership
changes affect you as
a principal?

Here are questions you can ask
yourself:

1. What kind of an end goal does the
   superintendent have for his/her career?
2. Does a search firm figure in those plans?
3. How old is your superintendent?
4. Does he/she want his/her children to stay in the same place?
5. Does the board have a history of stable superintendent relationships?
6. Which search firm is being used by the board for the search? What
   kind of "stock" does the firm have in its "stable"? (Some "stables"
   have "good ol' boys." Some have "golden boys.")
7. What kind of a superintendent helps me make the best use of my
   talents?

ACTIVITY 3.5

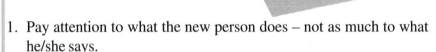

How do you maintain balance with leadership changing at the top?

Here are some strategies that seem to work when the top leadership is changing or unstable.

1. Pay attention to what the new person does – not as much to what he/she says.
2. Say less rather than more.
3. DO NOT CONFIDE IN COLLEAGUES about your fears or concerns. Quietly watch to see what he/she does.
4. When working with a new idea, send a person out (rather than yourself) to be the spokesperson. If the idea flies, you can give credit to the individual. If the idea doesn't, you can protect the person.
5. Keep a low profile until you can assess the new superintendent.
6. Work to make the best happen.
7. Provide open support for issues that you think are beneficial to the district.

Planning is important for principals. The template on the next page can be used vertically to help committees or groups work through design and implementation. There are some benefits, however, from making visual maps for everyone to see as you work through a plan. I learned this method from Suzanne Bailey, an educational and business consultant.

The full planning map is explained graphically. If the project is a long-term one, I use the entire planning model with much care. For a committee meeting or short-term projects, I will use only steps 5, 6, 7, and

8. In either case, the most important step is #5. If an outcome can be

clearly and precisely described, the chance of reaching it increases. One

time, in planning changes to a high school English curriculum, we spent a

month specifying the content, skills, and attitudes we wanted in Step #5.

THE GAME BOARD OF CHANGE

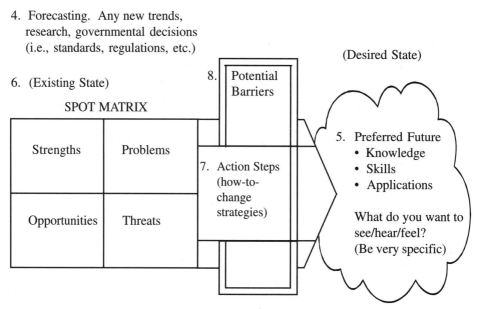

4. Forecasting. Any new trends, research, governmental decisions (i.e., standards, regulations, etc.)

(Desired State)

6. (Existing State)

SPOT MATRIX

8. Potential Barriers

Strengths	Problems
Opportunities	Threats

7. Action Steps (how-to-change strategies)

5. Preferred Future
   • Knowledge
   • Skills
   • Applications

   What do you want to see/hear/feel? (Be very specific)

1. Vertical slice of stakeholders or group(s) affected

2. History of Organization
   • "Prouds" and "sorries"
   • Key historical facts
   • Stories

3. Individual and/or organizational values, beliefs, guiding principles

9. Coaches' Corner

   What would my mentor/friend/confidant say?

   What would Suzanne Bailey tell me about this plan?

Adapted from Suzanne Bailey, Bailey Alliance (1995)

CHAPTER FOUR:
WALKING THE TIGHTROPE –
DEALING WITH CRISES
AND SAYING NO

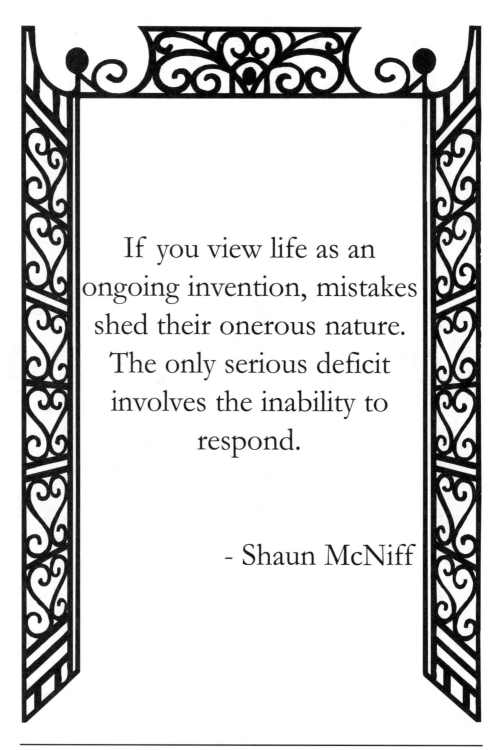

If you view life as an ongoing invention, mistakes shed their onerous nature. The only serious deficit involves the inability to respond.

\- Shaun McNiff

Conflict is. Living is conflict. When people get together or have to deal with their environment, there is conflict. Conflict can be destructive or constructive. As a new administrator I thought the goal was to have zero conflict. I kept thinking, "I must be doing something wrong." But as I matured I understood that the issue is not to get rid of conflict, the issue is to manage it so that it's productive. One strategy I use comes from a book called *Polarity Management* (1992) by Barry Johnson.

POLARITY MANAGEMENT

There are problems to solve and polarities to manage. Problems have a solution that ends the conflict. Polarities can be things like differences in pedagogy, innovation versus tradition, individual versus team. What is important to understand is that polarities have two positions that contribute positively to the organization. It is not to extinguish one side or the other. The requirements for a polarity that needs management are twofold:

1. The two poles are interdependent, <u>and</u> …
2. The issue is ongoing.

Richard Farson (*Management of the Absurd,* 1996) believes that 90% of the issues we deal with as administrators are polarities to manage, not problems to solve. He calls these polarities dilemmas. As we rethink some of the issues that plague us in schools, try to view them through the lens of polarity management.

Breathing becomes a good metaphor for meeting the two rules above. You need both an inhale and an exhale. It is hoped that these two are ongoing, or you probably wouldn't need to read any further. Let's look at another example.

In any school building there exists a group of staff members who want the most autonomy possible. They may be innovators or traditional in their approach, they may be young or old, but they want independence. At the same time, from a principal's viewpoint, there is a need for group cohesion and consensus on some issues. School goals or objectives come to mind. Even though you want individually strong staff, you also need the team concept. There are positives and negatives for both sides. It isn't about one or the other winning, it's about getting the positives of both.

POSITIVES AND NEGATIVES

Positives (individual)	Positives (team)
Individuality	Connectedness
Freedom	Belonging
Individual dreams and goals	Equality
Creativity	Shared vision
Efficacy	Team support
Negatives (individual)	Negatives (team)
Isolation	Sameness
Loss of equality	Excessive conformity
Loss of common direction and goals	Loss of individual dreams and goals
Loss of team support	Loss of individual initiative
Loss of team synergy	Loss of individual creativity
Selfishness	Group-think

Adapted from *Polarity Management* (1992)

Our goal, then, is to spend most of our time above the line, in the positive quadrants, and very little time below the line, in the negative quadrants. In some research this is called complementarity. It is "both/and" thinking; we need both in the organization. We need strong individuals and strong teams to make the organization strong and productive. No system will last very long performing on only one side of a polarity.

When the system slips into either lower quadrant, that is a sign to move diagonally to the positive side of the other pole. For principals this

provides a strategy to keep the system moving, productive, and striving to

get the positive outcomes for each group. When the principal stops

managing the poles, the system stagnates and is endangered.

This template may be written out for many issues we face. Crusaders

and tradition bearers, content and process, school and community,

behaviorism and humanism, etc.

ACTIVITY 4.1

Write out a polarity
quadrant on something you are
trying to manage. Remember, it has to be interdependent and ongoing.

RESPONSE STRATEGIES

As I reflected on my answer to my son's earlier question (p. 42), I

thought one of the most useful tools that support our tightrope trek across

the void is response strategies. These help you respond in real time, stop

the negative energy, and redirect thoughts into a generative mode. An

example in Chapter Three is the hockey story.

Besides having conflict-management strategies as a mental model, it

is important to have verbal ways to deal with conflict. Lynch and Kordis, in a book called *Strategy of the Dolphin* (1988), say it isn't what happens

to you, it's how you respond to what happens to you that determines the

quality of the conversation. I keep this list by the phone, since I always

seem to get at least one person who's upset on the phone during the day.

I used to keep this list posted by my doorframe because invariably I would

meet someone angry coming into my office just when I was trying to leave

my office.

Brain theory tells us that, when under stress or feeling under attack,

our brain is hijacked by the amygdala and goes to safety rather than

being in the neocortex where thinking occurs. To solve problems it's

extremely important to be able to think and consider all of your options.

This is very difficult when feeling under attack. The Reticular Activity

System (RAS) has worked very well for us for centuries, keeping us safe.

Unfortunately, the RAS can short-circuit our thinking. We also know

from Dan Goleman's work (1995) that the amygdala receives information 80,000 times faster than the neocortex. It's small wonder that it's hard to think clearly when we perceive that we're under attack.

Another prerequisite for handling emotional issues is as basic as breathing – literally. You must be able to breathe low in your diaphragm. It's necessary to get as much oxygen as possible to the brain in order to think more lucidly. Sometimes if someone who's angry is on the phone, I stand up and start to move. It helps me get more relaxed and in motion, rather than being static.

The response strategies I try to use are as follows:

1. **Be direct; use appropriate voice.**
2. **Paraphrase.**
3. **Silence, empathy, and non-judgmental acceptance.**
4. **Clarify; probe for specificity.**
5. **Chunking up.**
6. **Third position.**
7. **Three F's.**
8. **Dealing with people you can't stand.**
9. **Metaphor.**
10. **"I don't know."**

Each of these has some basic verbal or non-verbal skills that can be learned.

1. Be direct; use appropriate voice

The first strategy is responding directly using the correct voice pattern. When I say direct, I mean answer the question in a direct manner

and respond in the same representational system the questioner is

using. This means if they are speaking in visual language, respond in

visual language. The same goes for auditory and kinesthetic, too.

The voice pattern is another strategy I learned from Michael Grinder.

If you are making a comment that is a decision or you need people to

believe what you are saying, use the credible voice. This means the voice

will have a flat tone and will drop at the end. You must make sure you are

breathing low or credible will turn into anger. If you are asking for input

and want discussion, your voice will need to fluctuate more and will go up

at the end. This is called the approachable voice. Again, breathe low, or it

may come across as whining or pleading. Choose the voice pattern

appropriate for the message you want to deliver.

2. Paraphrase

Never underestimate the power of the paraphrase. As a former physics

teacher I didn't really know what a paraphrase was until I started coaching

others as an administrator. By paraphrasing you send a message that you

are listening, because you can't paraphrase if you haven't listened to the one who has been speaking.

The receiver knows intuitively that you are listening, and this is positive for the relationship. Also by paraphrasing it's an easy check to see if you have all the information that he/she thinks is important. If you miss some of the data, the other person will self-correct you without getting angry. Paraphrasing gives you time to think while you're making sure you have the correct information.

Make sure you don't "parrot-phrase." If you paraphrase by repeating exactly what the other person said, he/she will get tired quickly and may think you are mimicking him/her. Paraphrase is saying the major points in fewer words, checking to see if you understand. Remember, Stephen Covey (1989) talks about first understanding, then being understood.

Paraphrasing is also not saying the phrase, "I think I hear you saying," and then repeating everything that was just said. In trainings during the 1970s many of us were taught to preface our paraphrase with "I think I hear you saying" and then repeat what was said. I suggest you drop that stem so you don't send the wrong message. People don't like being "techniqued." If people think they're being techniqued, you may get results opposite from those you were seeking.

3. Silence, empathy, and non-judgmental acceptance

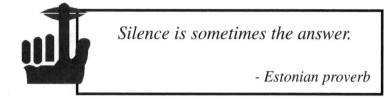

Silence is sometimes the answer.

- Estonian proverb

Silence. I try to make sure I listen to the speaker. Stephen Glenn, in

Developing Capable Young People (1985), says people want to be listened

to, taken seriously, and have a person be genuinely interested in them. By

being silent sometimes I can make sure I hear all of the issue rather than

getting into a debate or just waiting for my turn to respond. However, it's

important that you make sure the receiver knows you are listening. On the

phone that means you must make some noise so they know you are with

them. I sometimes say, "Uh-huh, OK, yes, sure, etc." In this way I can

spend time crafting a question that will help me understand, rather than

spending my time interrupting or escalating the disagreement.

Empathy. Sometimes people just want someone to empathize with

them. I ask people what role they want me to be in: coaching? advice-

giving? empathizing? just listening to you? This clarifies my role and

helps me provide the service the person is desiring without trying to guess.

David Perkins (1992) uses a term called "cognitive economy." We are all busy, and the more specific we can be saves time – and people get the

desired result.

Non-judgmental acceptance. I have found that, once I get defensive,

disagreements escalate fast. By remaining non-judgmental you can

discuss issues without agreeing.

Here are some phrases you can use ...

1. "Help me understand how you came to that conclusion."
2. "I will accept differences of opinion. But destruction of relationships in this building is not acceptable."
3. "I know you love your children ..."
4. "I know we want the best for your child. How can we support that happening?"
5. "In this building, children are not allowed to do it, and neither are adults."
6. "The rules that allow you to meet allow them to meet. Everyone has equal access."
7. "I appreciate that you advocate for your child. I advocate for all the students in the building. So my perspective is different."
8. "The safety and security of each child in this building are of the utmost importance. I'm sure you can understand and support that."
9. "I want to thank you for having the courage to call me. You have helped me get ahead of the game."

I urge caution by using the term "yes" as a way of signifying you

agree. In many cultures "yes" means you hear them, you understand

them. In most Western cultures "yes" means agreement. Keep in mind,

too, that praise usually signals – and singles out – conformity. Praise sometimes feels manipulative. See Alfie Kohn's work *Punished by Rewards* (1993) for research on praise and rewards.

4. Clarify; probe for specificity

Susan Forward, in her book *Emotional Blackmail* (1996), talks about a pattern of conversations that usually end up in compliance or hostility. A parent, or another stakeholder, makes a demand on the principal. The principal resists. The parent puts the pressure on, the principal resists. The parent now threatens the principal. The principal moves either to comply with the demand or digs in to a win/lose stance. Neither result is win/win, and neither preserves the relationship.

Forward recommends that at the first demand you start asking for specifics, i.e., who, what, where, why, when. Intervene at the earliest possible opportunity. The farther along the process, the fewer options you have. The key is challenging any assumptions or presuppositions made by the demand. Get specific data, or you might be answering the wrong question.

There is a tool called the Meta Model that also is effective in surfacing covert issues. You may find a more complete description in a book by Genie LaBorde called *Influencing with Integrity* (1983).

Basically it's a way to ask questions or challenge assumptions and language that use generalizations, deletions, and distortions. When you hear fuzzy nouns or verbs, the challenge is *which* teachers, administrators, students, parents, et al., specifically? When a fuzzy verb is used, the challenge question is how specifically? How will you know specifically? How will they understand specifically? Words like "always," "never," and "everybody" are universal quantifiers. The way to get specificity from those statements is threefold. First, you try intonation: *Everybody?* If that doesn't work, go for exaggeration: *Everybody in the whole school has one?* And finally you can go for exception: *Is there anyone who doesn't have one?* That usually will cut through most generalizations. When comparators are used, such as ... "I buy Toyotas because they're better" or "I buy Raisin Bran because I get 50% more" ... it's important to ask the question – compared to what? Advertisers use all of the above to sell their products.

5. Chunking up

A good way to find agreement is chunking up.

Sometimes in discussions you may have to move up to find agreement

on something, anything. Once you have agreement on an overarching

issue, it's easier to find ways to agree on other things. For instance, a

student is having difficulty in a class. The argument is over attendance,

assignments, etc. When you say, "We all want Mary to be successful and

graduate from school," the parents will agree because that's what they

want, too. Once you hear the word "yes" or see a head nod, then ask,

"What are some of the options we can think of that will help Mary be

successful?" Or: "How might we work together so Mary will be success

ful?" This invites participation in a constructive manner, rather than con-

tinuing a discussion over a rule or opinion.

6. Third position

Again, I learned the concept of going to third position from Michael

Grinder, national director of NeuroLinguistic Programming in Education.

This strategy can use grade books, handbooks, white board, or anything

that can serve as a third point. Sometimes you look at that third position

and talk about it rather than keeping eye contact with the person, which

tends to make everything personal between the two people. Using the third position helps keep personal attacks reduced and the focus on the

issue. It's important to establish a third-position visual, talk in specifics,

and keep eye contact on the third position while interpreting information.

Look at the person when generating options to help the situation.

7. Three F's *F F F*

I have used the Three F's when I have changed my mind or a

person may be dealing with old information. It goes like this: Felt –

Found – Feel. I **felt** that way at one time, but I **found** out ... and now I

feel ... An example: At one time I felt that special-education students

should be separated from the mainstream. But I found out that both

special-education students and mainstream students benefit from working

with diversity and thereby learn how to deal with each other better. Now I

feel it's important to mainstream students. Just fill in the specific issue.

It's a way to rechannel negative energy into a positive direction.

8. Dealing with people you can't stand

Brinkman & Kirschner wrote a book titled *Dealing with People You*

Can't Stand (1994); it gives a template that can be helpful in many situa-

tions. If you can figure out which quadrant the person is in, it helps to determine how to respond to his/her needs. People tend to fall into four "get" categories. Some want to get things done, some want to get things right, some want to get along with others, and some want to get appreciated. Knowing which is the most important helps you respond appropriately and reduce the time spent guessing. This book does give additional strategies for each quadrant.

9. Metaphor

Some people enjoy talking in metaphor. One person I had a lot of contact with always talked about fishing. We could communicate through the metaphor of fishing, even though we both knew we were talking about his son's teachers. Since metaphors cause higher-level thinking, it takes time for the person to respond. This can give you a break to collect your thoughts. I suggest you include books of proverbs, quotes, and/or sayings when you read books and articles. Three of my favorites are ... African proverb: "Not learning is bad; not wanting to learn is worse" ... Chinese proverb: "It is easier to stay out than get out" ... and French proverb: "Children need models more than critics." Metaphors speak to both sides of the brain and normally will cause a different kind of thinking process.

10. "I don't know"

After the straightforward comment "I don't know," I use such follow-up statements as: (1) "Does anyone else know?" (2) "I will find out and get back to you"; or (3) "But what I do know about the subject is ..." I'm sure you have others. What follow-up statements can you think of?

ACTIVITY 4.2

1. Think of a recent discussion or attack where one of these 10 approaches could have been useful.
2. How would you have responded using one of these tools?

Another tool I have used with individuals, pairs, small groups, and large groups is a model I learned from Bob Chadwick. It goes as follows:

GROUP-PROCESS QUESTIONS

I. Grounding
    A. What is the issue and your connection to it?
    B. How do you feel about it?
II. Process/Elaboration
    A. What is the worst possible outcome if you do or don't change?
    B. What is the best possible outcome if you do or don't change?
III. Application
    A. What strategies and/or actions will foster the best possible outcomes?

   B. What values and beliefs will lead to actions that foster
    the best possible outcomes?
   C. What actions are you committed to taking?

Adapted from Bob Chadwick (1997)

VOICES

Part of resolving and dealing with crisis is using the adult voice.

THREE VOICES

---

* <u>THE CHILD VOICE</u>: defensive, victimized, emotional, whining,
 losing attitude, strongly negative non-verbal

 ~ Quit picking on me.
 ~ You don't love me.
 ~ You want me to leave.
 ~ Nobody likes (loves) me.
 ~ I hate you.
 ~ You're ugly.
 ~ You make me sick.
 ~ It's your fault.
 ~ Don't blame me.
 ~ She, he, ... did it.
 ~ You make me mad.
 ~ You made me do it.

* *The child voice is also playful, spontaneous, curious, etc. The*
 phrases listed often occur in conflictual or manipulative situations
 and impede resolution.

THREE VOICES

---

* **   THE PARENT VOICE: authoritative, directive, judgmental, evaluative, win-lose mentality, demanding, punitive, sometimes threatening

---

> ~ You shouldn't (should) do that.
> ~ It's wrong (right) to do ....
> ~ That's stupid, immature, out of line, ridiculous.
> ~ Life's not fair. Get busy.
> ~ You are good, bad, worthless, beautiful (any judgmental, evaluative comment).
> ~ You do as I say.
> ~ If you weren't so ...., this wouldn't happen to you.
> ~ Why can't you be like ....?

*   *The parent voice can also be very loving and supportive. The phrases listed usually occur during conflict and impede resolution.*

**   *The internal parent voice can create shame and guilt.*

THREE VOICES

THE ADULT VOICE: non-judgmental, free of negative non-verbal, factual, often in question format, attitude of win-win

~ In what ways could this be resolved?
~ What factors will be used to determine the effectiveness, quality of ....?
~ I would like to recommend ....
~ What are choices in this situation?
~ I am comfortable (uncomfortable) with ....
~ Options that could be considered are ....
~ For me to be comfortable, I need the following things to occur ....
~ These are the consequences of that choice/action ....
~ We agree to disagree.

EMOTIONAL/MENTAL MODELS

Another factor affecting both communication and learning is emotion.

How people (students, parents, teachers and, yes principals) feel makes a

big difference in how we communicate, as well as learn (see chart on next

page). Remember, all learning is double-coded – both mentally and

emotionally.

EMOTIONAL/MENTAL MODELS *

Stage	Cognitive	Emotional	May Not Be Fully Developed If …
Stage 1: Ability to attend	• Focuses on sensory data that come from relationships • Finds patterns in sensations	• Calms self internally to focus on sensations • Establishes order from patterns	• Attention is fleeting • Very active or agitated • Self-absorbed, passive
Stage 2: Ability to engage	• Relates sensory data to feelings	• Creates feelings of intimacy • Relates to response	• Need-oriented • Aloof, withdrawn • Lack of intimacy • Strong emotions can disrupt caring
Stage 3: Ability to be intentional	• Uses non-verbals with purpose and intention	• Creates and directs desire	• Lacks full range of emotional expression • Aimless, fragmented behaviors • No larger social goals
Stage 4: Ability to form complex inter-active patterns	• Purposefully interacts with others to negotiate and receive approval and acceptance	• Elicits range of desired feelings	• Misreads intentions and assigns causes to suspicion, mistreatment, etc. • Cannot read subtle cues
Stage 5: Ability to create images, symbols, ideas (verbal)	• Gives meaning to abstract mental constructs	• Assigns feelings to mental constructs (mind is fragmented without this)	• Ideas are concrete • Translates ideas to actions • Discusses some feelings but not full range of feelings
Stage 6: Ability to connect images, symbols, and ideas	• Develops abstract architecture	• Can "image" feel-ings/desires with mental constructs • Embeds emotion and meaning	• Ideas are fragmented and disconnected • Polarized thinking • Thinking is constricted

* Adapted from work of Stanley Greenspan, M.D. (1997). *The Growth of the Mind and the Endangered Origins of Intelligence.*

What are the mental models you have as a principal? Sketch a picture

of the following:

~ How you feel when you are criticized.
~ How you feel when you have an angry parent.

Can you change your emotional/mental models? *Should* you change

them?

VERBAL ABUSE

In communication it is important to note verbal abuse. It is subtle,

insidious, vague, and extremely damaging. When a principal is a victim

of verbal abuse, it is difficult to identify. Verbal abuse is psychological

violence.

Verbal abuse is a roller coaster between compliment and criticism. It

is unpredictable, manipulative, and controlling – and frequently carries a

double message. Patricia Evans, in her book *The Verbally Abusive*

Relationship (1996), identifies categories of verbal abuse. These catego-

ries are: withholding (going into silence), countering, discounting, hurtful

comments disguised as jokes, blocking and diverting, accusing and

blaming, judging and criticizing, trivializing, undermining, threatening,

name-calling, forgetting, ordering, denial, abusive anger.

Withholding: The individual keeps his/her thoughts to him/herself and remains silent and aloof. Examples: "There's nothing to talk about." "You wouldn't be interested." "Why should I tell you? You don't care anyway; you're an administrator."

Countering: The individual indicates that what was observed wasn't so. Sample exchange ... Administrator: "When you did the lesson about time, all the students seemed to know the lesson." Teacher: "You've never taught kindergarten, so you wouldn't know." Administrator: "What do you look for to know if students are learning?" Teacher: "Why are you asking me? You should know."

Discounting: The individual denies and distorts the perception of the other person. Examples: "You're too sensitive." "You're not tough enough on these kids." "You don't know what you're talking about."

Hurtful comments disguised as jokes: "Well, what can you expect from an administrator?" "People who can't teach become principals."

Blocking and diverting: Comments all used to stop or prevent communication or to withhold information. Examples: "Who died and made you God?" "Get off my back." "You have to have the last word!" Diverting occurs when information is asked for, and there is no response.

For example, if the question is asked, "What happened in the parent/

teacher conference?" responses could be: "Don't you trust me?"

"You believe the parents before you believe me!"

Accusing and blaming occur when an individual assigns blame

based on some real or imagined wrongdoing – or to take the focus off the

person: "It's your fault these kids are allowed to misbehave." "If you had

a good discipline plan, this wouldn't happen." "You always let parents

make the decisions."

Judging and criticizing occur when comments are made about the

person in a critical, judgmental way – either to his/her face or to others:

"The problem with you is ..." "He/she never does what he/she says ..."

"He/she can't find his/her way out of a paper bag." Judging and criticizing

are often disguised as advice: "Wouldn't it have been better if ..." "Why

don't you just make a decision?"

Trivializing is when an individual says through non-verbals or

verbals that what you have done is insignificant: "I realize that

administrators don't do anything but drink coffee. But just today, don't

you think you could take a minute and ..."

Undermining dampens enthusiasm: "When are you retiring?" "Who asked you?" "You wouldn't understand." "Someone promised you a job."

Threatening is informing that there will be loss or pain: "If you can't get this for me, I won't help with the after-school program."

Name-calling is simply that. **Forgetting** is often a form of manipulation. **Ordering** (giving a direction), **denial**, and **abusive anger** are self-explanatory.

CHAPTER FIVE:
CLIMBING THE MOUNTAIN –
MOVING YOUR ANCHOR

The reasonable man adapts himself to the world; the unreasonable one persists in trying to adapt the world to himself. Therefore, all progress depends on the unreasonable man.

- George Bernard Shaw

To continue moving toward goals, it becomes important to move your anchors to other locations. The anchor does not change – just its location and the angle at which it is embedded.

To move toward goals, one of the activities that must be engaged in is planning. Planning in the form of stories or scenarios is one way Royal Dutch Shell dealt with the oil embargo of the 1970s.

SCENARIO PLANNING

One planning strategy that is used in the business world, but not much in education, is scenario planning. Peter Schwartz (1996), Arie de Geus (1997), and others have used this model successfully to help determine future probable scenarios. This gives organizations a head start when the environment changes rapidly. The process goes as follows:

First, get a diverse group of people in the room to provide a wide perspective. The partnerships that can be established – e.g., administrators and union representatives, business and school representatives, social agencies and ancillary services – may provide the foundation for solving issues in a more systemic way.

Second, identify trends that are on the horizon. Technology comes to mind, vouchers are affecting public schools in some states, and home-schooling seems to be a trend. It's important to surface as many future possibilities as possible.

Third, articulate what is known about the future. In some states standards are the current driving force. Other states are dealing with technology issues. Identify what we know at the present time.

Fourth, identify what we don't know, the unknowns. Having the group name the unknowns starts people thinking about the future and the uncertainty that may lie ahead. From that list of unknowns the group needs to vote on the top two biggest concerns. You may want to reduce the list to five or six first and then finally vote on the two primary unknowns. In one group I worked with, the two unknowns were the impact of technology and the impact of standards on the curriculum and school structure. Once the two unknowns are determined, they become

the two axes of a quadrant. For example:

<u>Impact of Technology</u>
High

High tech, low standards	High tech, high standards
Low tech, low standards	Low tech, high standards

<u>Impact of Standards</u>

Low

High

Low

Fifth, write a scenario of each of those possibilities. Develop a school

that has each of the four as an outcome in order to establish what impact

they may have on the school culture, people, and programs. Identify the

key skeletal characteristics of the combinations of dimensions. It's

important to write a general description of all four because all four are

possibilities.

Sixth, pick two of the most probable or preferable scenarios and

develop them more fully with as much detail as possible. Usually the two that people pick are the most desirable. After group members identify the

most desirable scenarios, they start developing action plans to obtain

the best possible outcomes.

ACTIVITY 5.1

Use scenarios in planning
for future issues.

GUT-LEVEL OR INTUITIVE PLANNING

*We have paid a drastic price
for trying to disconnect
emotions from intellect.*

- Robert Cooper

Think of the time and energy we have spent trying to make a science

out of teaching or making teaching teacher-proof. When we tried to make

teaching a step-by-step process, some of my best teachers did not do any

of the things research said to do. On the other hand, I saw teachers do

every one of the steps and still not produce good instruction. The problem

with trying to make teaching routine is that teaching is both science and art.

As Goleman (1995) and Cooper and Sawaf (1997) write, having

emotional intelligence is bringing the knowledge base and the intuitive

information together for the best teaching. Intuition has been identified as

creative wisdom: "We just felt it was the proper thing to do." Many

people say they felt something intuitively well before the data or behavior

said it was the right way to go. In order to have elegant teaching,

learning, and administrating we must have both IQ and EQ. We need the

head *and* the heart to lead and manage complex educational systems.

I predict that leadership-training institutions in the future will devote

more and more time to intuition and creativity on the job and in planning

sessions. In the Western world we have some great rational thinkers and

rational processes that have been used effectively over the years. If

rational thought would have solved all of our problems in education, I

think we would have already succeeded. It is time to add value to

decision-making and leadership by increasing our potential on the

emotional, intuitive side.

OUTCOME MAPPING

This is a backwards planning process. In essence you "begin with the

end in mind" (Covey, 1989). On a piece of paper on the right side, write down what your goal or objective might be – e.g., helping administrators

deal with conflict more effectively.

Help Adm deal with conflict more effectively

Second, to the left, write down the knowledge, skills, and attitudes

(KSAs) administrators need in order to deal more effectively with conflict.

Knowledge 　*Getting to YES* 　Polarity management 　Response strategies Skills 　Breathing 　Voice patterns 　Going visual 　Third position Attitudes 　Want to get better 　Reduce stress	Help Adm deal with conflict more effectively

Third, again to the left of the first two columns, write down what you ind-

ividually need to model or the goals and objectives you have for yourself.

Individual Goals 　Model conflict- 　management 　strategies in my 　day-to-day 　behavior	Knowledge 　*Getting to YES* 　Polarity manage- 　　ment 　Response strategies Skills 　Breathing 　Voice patterns 　Going visual 　Third position Attitudes 　Want to get better 　Reduce stress	Help Adm deal with conflict more effectively

Finally, what KSAs do you need, individually, in order to model these strategies in the workplace?

Individual KSAs	Individual Goals	Knowledge	Help Adm deal with

Knowledge
    Read *Getting to YES*
    Read *Getting Past NO*
    Read *Magic of Conflict*
 	
Skills
    Practice polarity management
    Take training in Chadwick process
 	
Attitudes
    Be positive about conflict
    Encourage others to be proactive about conflict
	Model conflict-management strategies in my day-to-day behavior	*Getting to YES*
		    Polarity management
		    Response strategies
		
		Skills
		    Breathing
		    Voice patterns
		    Going visual
		    Third position
		
		Attitudes
		    Want to get better
		    Reduce stress
			conflict more effectively

This process is a way to start with a wider goal but with specific steps on how to get to that outcome – what the individual must do to promote results, as well as identification of learning required to behave differently.

PLANNING BACKWARDS

Planning backwards can be used to lay out timelines. Simply draw a calendar frame, go to the due date or implementation date, and work backwards. It works extremely well.

Monday	Tuesday	Wednesday	Thursday	Friday	Saturday	Sunday
				Compute date		
Secretary keyboards		Committee	Report due			

While this example is an oversimplification, the planner started on

Friday when it was due and worked backwards.

USING HARD DATA

This is an excellent method for making change and riding out change.

If you can show through hard data (quantifiable and provable) that the

change is needed or is working, the change will come faster.

MAKING MISTAKES

The issue is not if you will make mistakes. You will. The issue is

twofold: What can I learn from my mistakes, and can they be repaired? If

so, how?

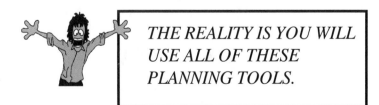

*THE REALITY IS YOU WILL
USE ALL OF THESE
PLANNING TOOLS.*

Fail small, fast, and forward.

- Tom Peters

Recovery is more important
than perfection.

- Michael Grinder

CHAPTER SIX:
ANCHOR OF IDENTITY

Who are you? Part of dealing with the principalship is knowing your bottom line. These are questions you must answer in your own mind. This activity could anchor you in the roughest of weather.

ACTIVITY 6.1

When push comes to shove, who am I at the core of my being?

1. Over what issues would I be willing to be fired or resign?
2. What decisions that I make that are reversed by someone above me would cause me to leave?
3. What do I give my time priorities to?
4. What criticisms (founded or unfounded) about me bother me the most?
5. What parts of the job am I willing to leave undone?
6. What things am I not willing to give up? For example, job security, promotion possibilities, the well-being of students, faculty happiness, union support, parental support, superintendent support, the camaraderie of other principals, student achievement.
7. What manipulations, dishonesties, "unfairnesses," omissions, and straight-out lies bother me the most?
8. What am I most willing to forgive and forget?
9. What would I never change about myself?
10. What are some things I like about myself?

In addition to who you are at your very essence, you are further defined by the identities of those around you. Your context (or environment of other entities and their needs) often is a very high determinant of success in a particular institution.

ACTIVITY 6.2

Who are the people around you?

1. Who evaluates me?
   What is their bottom line? In other words, what would they take a stand for or against even if they were fired for that stand?
2. Who is your superintendent? What is his/her bottom line? How much support does he/she have on the board? How long has he/she been in the community?
3. Who is on your school board? How stable is the school board? Who are the power brokers in the community they represent? (Chapter Two has techniques for identifying the power brokers.)
4. Who are your teachers? Are any of them a key spokesperson for the union?
5. Who was your predecessor? What was his/her bottom line?
6. Why were you brought into this situation? What previous situation occurred that you are to modify or correct?
7. Who are your school's parents and what are their expectations?
8. Who are the key players in the central-office infrastructure? Who in the central office can help you and in what ways? Who wants to hinder you and in what ways? (See Chapter Two for analytical tools.)
9. Who are your students? What do they need? How will you know?
10. Who are your friendly critics or critical friends who will tell you what you may not want to hear?

Pity the poor leader who has unfriendly critics and uncritical friends.
                                        - John Gardner

After reviewing your responses to those two sets of questions, answer the following questions.

ACTIVITY 6.3

Focus of identity:

1. What is my bottom line? What am I willing to be fired for and where would I like to focus my time?
2. When I take the stand I identified in #1 and allocate my time as I identified in #1, what will be the criticisms and reactions from each of the above groups?
3. Can you live with the criticisms and/or political fallout?
4. Can you use the tools in Chapter Five to deal with the crises that result?

Not all of these questions can be answered definitively every time because each situation has nuances and differences. However, when you are clear about the majority of these answers, a vital anchor has been established.

MY BOTTOM LINE IS:

What will I go to the wall for?

WHAT DOES YOUR SCHOOL BOARD WANT?

In most of the world, the educational system is managed by a central authority. The system has a minister of education or someone who determines what is taught and when. In the United States and Canada, school boards are elected to set policy concerning schools. In most cases seven people are elected to oversee the school district's mission. Unfortunately, the seven members sometimes are concerned about seven or more different things. All too often election outcomes are determined because a group of people is angry about one issue. Other board members are elected based on whether they support the current superintendent. Some are wrestling with open enrollment, test scores, etc. School boards would do well to remember a quote by John Dewey:

> *What the best and wisest parents want for [their] child is what the country should want for [its] children.*
>
> *- John Dewey*

Sometimes in an effort to get what a school-board member wants –

or what the group who helped get that person elected wants – folks forget

what is good for everyone's children. School boards want to get their

issues resolved, and they want happy parents. As a principal you have to

determine if the demands, changes, or requests from the school board

(sometimes through the central office) are the right things to do. In the

final analysis, the principal has to do what he/she thinks is right. Such

decisions are based on your own beliefs and values, your own knowledge

base, and your own experience. This is why the principal's identity is so

important. Your identity is based on your beliefs and values.

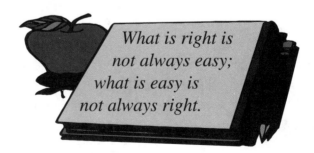

*What is right is
not always easy;
what is easy is
not always right.*

School boards want their constituents happy, and they want the district employees to carry out their desires efficiently and effectively. This is not always possible. In a case where the Board of Education decided to build a 3,200-student high school, there were people against a school that size. Even though research shows that, in a school of more than 1,600, students feel less connected to school, student achievement is reduced, violence increases, and supervision becomes more problematic, the board voted to build it.

Soon, of course, many of the issues began coming to the surface. The principal in this school felt very strongly that the new school should not be built. However, once the decision was made, the principal directed his efforts to planning and implementing the best way he knew how. I applaud this principal for being able to put the issue behind him and moving on. Some principals cannot or will not do that and end up causing themselves and others a lot of grief.

In the final analysis, our system says school boards get to make policy decisions. That is their right and obligation. The principal must be ready to take a stand on the issues but also be willing to close ranks in support of a decision. There also are cases, when a principal's principles are at stake, that resignation is the best alternative, rather than a pattern of sniping from

the sidelines.

WHAT DOES YOUR SUPERINTENDENT WANT?

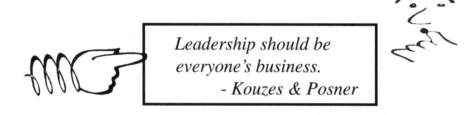

> *Leadership should be*
> *everyone's business.*
> *- Kouzes & Posner*

Superintendents, like principals, are between political forces that

sometimes are in conflict. The role of the superintendent is to administra-

tively carry out the policies set by the Board of Education. They also must

develop relationships with the many facets and factions of the community.

The #1 allegiance of the superintendent is answering to the Board of

Education. The board chooses the superintendent, directs the superinten-

dent, and evaluates the superintendent.

The next priority is the central-office administrators who report di-

rectly to the superintendent. It is the delegation of the administrative

function that facilitates work getting done. The superintendent in some

districts will have direct responsibility for principals, but in every district

there is at least some indirect responsibility for the principals. Many

issues that superintendents deal with are a direct result of what happens in
the school building headed by the principal. This means superintendents
need direct or indirect information from the building sites in order to
answer questions resulting from decisions made.

Superintendents need information and possible consequences regarding those decisions from central-office staff
and principals. Some want honesty, some want only good
news, and some want creative thinking. The principal must
evaluate whether to give the superintendent "what they want"
and/or "what they need." This can be a political decision.
The principal must be clear on what information he/she will
give and why. Principals need to act with intentionality to
make conscious choices about what and how they interact
with the superintendent.

The superintendent can be an invaluable resource for principals. Superintendents can provide (1) safety for a principal, enabling him/her to take
risks; (2) unfiltered feedback to the principal, which will result in more
learning and development; and (3) career counseling. This is true of
central-office personnel as well. They can guide, mentor, and model team-

work for principals in the field. Principals will be watching to see how central-office administrators handle conflict and disagreements – as examples of theory in practice.

Superintendents who choose to make political decisions for their own safety can find themselves at odds with practitioners. This tightrope must have two anchor points. If either one starts to lose its foundation, the superintendent might find walking very unstable. Both ends, such as the board and the district, must have sturdy foundations in order for the walk to be secure. Dealing with change, therefore, can be very uncomfortable at times.

WHAT DO TEACHERS WANT?

The good news is there are many different teachers wanting many different things. The bad news is there are many different teachers wanting many different things. In a world of increasing diversity in thought, ethnicity, instructional strategies, and assessment tools, we want efficacious teachers who can make decisions and demonstrate leadership in the school structure. At the same time principals are judged on their ability to provide a vision for the school, model that vision, and keep the diverse segments working toward common goals. Teachers want the security of shared group norms while maintaining their own individuality. This is an ongoing management dilemma, as Barry Johnson discusses in *Polarity Management* (1992). These are poles to manage, not determining the one right way.

Teachers want flexibility within their own classroom while keeping the school safe. Unfortunately, these two concepts are in conflict at times. In an urban setting, security of the school sometimes will supersede the ability to be open and have staff and students be able to get out into the community. Occasionally, too, because of limited space, the ability to do large groups can be reduced.

Teachers also want to know someone is in charge – by being a leader, a manager, or a combination of both. Staff members need to know that the budgets, schedules, staffing, etc., are being handled. They also want to know there is a vision, a plan for school improvement. The principal has a responsibility to keep hope alive.

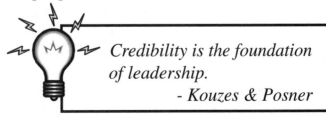

Credibility is the foundation of leadership.
- Kouzes & Posner

Credibility is another attribute staff members want in their leaders.

Without integrity there is no moral anchor to build relationships. In the

field of education, as in many other institutions, relationships are the

building blocks of organizations. Credibility, of course, is the intersection

of the principal's talk and walk. Congruence between what is said and

what is done is normally the test of credibility. Teachers want to see

modeling of the behavior that is expected of them.

WHAT DO PARENTS WANT?

> *There is no more important deliberation
> confronting us than how we, both as
> individuals and as a society, will raise
> our children.*
>
> *- David Walsh*

Parents want to be heard. The recent history of schools has included

site councils, budgetary committees, long-range planning, and foundations

– to name a few. All of the groups have a purpose of incorporating parents

and communities into the policy-making and operations of the school. One

operating metaphor for the future of schools with parents is partnership.

Adversarial relationships will not produce the results we need to lead complex systems. We'll need all segments of the organization to work in partnership in order to produce successful learners.

Sometimes, however, parents think input equals decision-making. Input does not necessarily mean decision-making. As principal you are responsible for the budget, staffing, etc. You cannot shift that responsibility to others. There are many techniques to use in order to bring groups into the process. But the final decisions will remain with the principal at the building level. Otherwise, the most vocal groups may get more attention, staffing, and budget than groups without advocates. This could lead to inequities, especially between the "haves" and the "have-nots." A principal needs to make every effort to ensure that all students are provided for in the school community. A principal also needs to ensure that all parents in the community have input – whether or not they are vocal about having influence.

WHAT DO STUDENTS WANT?

Children are the purpose of life. We were once children, and someone cared for us. Now it is our time to care.

- Cree elder

This is a hard question because of the multiple possibilities. The answer may depend upon how many students you have in your school. Stephen Glenn, in *Developing Capable Young People* (1985), says children want to be listened to and taken seriously – and to have a genuine interest shown in their well-being. Even when I don't agree with students, maintaining their dignity is of the utmost importance. Most of us can talk about hard issues if we feel we're being treated respectfully.

I hear a lot of talk about fairness. But fairness, like beauty, is in the eye of the beholder. Sometimes adults use the statement "Life is not fair." This is where listening can make all the difference. Being listened to is affirming. Being treated fairly is the issue, because not everyone is going to get exactly what everyone else gets.

Students also want to know that adults in the building have their best interests in mind. This means students will be prepared for future endeavors, staff cares about students, and someone will help them with their problems. Most of this comes back to relationships. Schools will be judged based on the relationships among all the participants in the school culture.

WHO EVALUATES YOU?

Everyone. Of course, there is the formal process. But generally speaking, the formal process is not how principals are evaluated. The informal process from constituents is most important. Principals are under constant supervision by everyone. This is why modeling and congruence are so essential.

There is another viewpoint, however, that is extremely important. That is the internal evaluation process. Robert Cooper states that 46% of all workers eventually leave because they don't feel appreciated. Teachers are isolated, but even more so are principals. If you evaluate yourself based on external feedback, you may well not feel appreciated.

This is why it's useful to have an internal evaluation system and internal feedback system. Journaling, having a coach to talk to, meditation, exercise, whatever will provide the internal structures … all can be helpful in increasing and sustaining the principal's emotional intelligence.

FUDs

Nothing is more harmful to a positive, creative attitude than fears, uncertainties, and doubts (FUDs); yet, most people let FUDs control their lives.

- Michael Mikado

It's vital that principals limit the impact of FUDs on their professional and personal life. If we allow ourselves to be preoccupied with FUDs, we won't be able to apply full mental and physical energy to the leadership issues at hand. Psychologists indicate that two basic belief patterns – internal and external – are necessary to reduce the impact of FUDs on our life. First, principals must believe internally that they are adequate, can handle the job of being principal, and can do the tasks at hand. They need to know they are responsible and independent enough to manage and lead the school site. Second, they need to know they have external equity – that they are as talented and adaptable as other professionals in their job category. Principals must believe they are at least as good as principals in other districts.

ACTIVITY 6.4

1. What fears, uncertainties, and doubts existed in your past professional positions?
2. How did you effectively deal with those FUDs?
3. What FUDs exist in your current position?
4. What internal and external resources do you have or need in order to successfully address the current demands of your position?
5. Where might you find additional resources?

I never take counsel of my fears.

- Gen. George Patton

ACTIVITY 6.5

Finish the story:

Once upon a time there was a principal named _____ who worked in a school called _____. The principal found greatest satisfaction in the school when _____. He/she was able to structure the time to do this by giving up _____. The principal was bothered when people made comments about _____. One thing the principal worried about was his/her ability to _____. An uncertainty that bothered the principal was _____, and he/she occasionally doubted _____. When students were interviewed about this principal, they used these terms: _____, _____, and _____. The principal smiled when he/she thought of students who _____. The thing he/she did that made the biggest difference in his/her school was _____. Although parents didn't always agree, they always believed that he/she stood for _____. When teachers talked among themselves about the principal, they used the following phrases: _____, _____, and _____. One of the stories the teachers told was about the time _____. Other principals in the district always remarked about _____ when they discussed him/her. Central office referred to this principal as _____. In the community this principal was known for _____. When an issue came to the board table involving this building or principal, the board would ask _____. The board decisions did (did not) reflect the recommendations of the principal. When asked about this principal by a news reporter, the superintendent said: _____ _____.

CHAPTER SEVEN:
MAINTAINING YOUR TIGHTROPE –
SELF-RENEWAL

I have accepted fear
as part of my warm-up;
it plays an important role
in stirring creative energy.

- Shaun McNiff

The hours are long and the job thankless. How do you keep the tightrope taut and the walk steady?

Schools and districts have been "fad-surfing" for many years. We go from program to program trying to find the holy grail of processes to install in our school that will solve our problems. This fad-surfing continues to be popular, but it diverts us from the long-term improvement of learning. Every new program takes time, money, and energy to initiate. When results are not immediate, we dump it and try another. There is always an implementation dip for anything new. It's important to stay with programs, collect data, analyze what is happening, and then make decisions. As long as we keep jumping from one panacea to another, long-term sustained change will be difficult, if not impossible, to attain.

Howard McCluskey has a theory on adult learning. It's called Theory of Margin. People don't have perfect control over their lives, and in schools you always must be prepared for the unexpected and live with ambiguity. The "margin" is the ratio of the relationship between "load" (the personal and social demands required to do the job with a minimum level of autonomy) and "power" (the resources). The external load consists of tasks involved in normal life requirements (family, work, and community responsibilities), while the internal load consists of life expectancies developed by people (aspirations, desires, and future expectations). Power is a combination of external resources, e.g., family, social, and financial, as well as internal resources: accumulated skills and experience.

There are two primary choices in dealing with the "margin": It can be increased either by reducing load or increasing power. Sometimes surplus power is needed to provide a cushion to meet various emergencies.

Balancing the demands requires some sort of margin. Principals need to help themselves and staff discover resources to deal with the increasing loads. It will be crucial to develop surpluses of power (resources) because of the element of surprise and intensity of today's issues.

ACTIVITY 7.1

What is your load, and what are your power readings?

	Internal	External
Load		
Power		

Some techniques that make a difference in self-renewal are the

following:

1. Finding a coach
2. Identifying your favorite activities
3. Sapping and zapping
4. Grieving
5. Celebrating transitions.
6. Maintaining perspective – core values
7. Becoming your own coach

These help reduce load and/or increase power.

FINDING A COACH

Another idea that can help you survive in the principalship is finding

a good coach. More and more business managers, CEOs, and

superintendents are finding coaches to help them lead in complex systems.

To coach and be coached can develop a reciprocal relationship that can help both people. I know of a person who coaches a superintendent because that position is very isolated. Who does a superintendent talk to? It's hard to get unfiltered feedback or suggestions for improvement from people without a political agenda.

Finding a coach may be difficult, but there are eligible individuals in your personal or professional life. I find these people from common interest groups. When I meet other learners who are interested in their own learning, as well as that of others, who read books, who attend workshops to increase their skills, I pay attention to them. I may want to travel in their pack, I may want to pick their brain, and I may want to develop a relationship. With time and trust, this may be a person who could serve as a coach.

Sometimes, though, it might be someone from out of town or a mentor from one's past. Eventually, we need to talk to someone about our plans and what is happening in our life – and to reflect back on events to gain from the experience. This involves a coach whom you can trust, who is confidential, and who will give you caring but honest feedback. These people are hard to come by, but they're very important to your mental health.

IDENTIFYING YOUR FAVORITE ACTIVITIES

Keeping balance in your personal and professional life is

vital. So, keep a sense of humor and have a private life. The following

exercise may help remind you to be good to yourself.

ACTIVITY 7.2

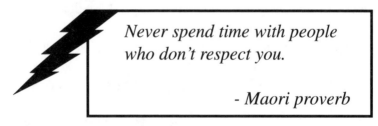

1. Write 10 things you
    like to do.
2. Jot down how much time you
    spend a week doing those things.
3. Compare the things you like to do
    with the time spent actually doing things you like.
4. What are you noticing about this comparison?
5. How would you change the amount of time to accommodate things
    that you like to do and therefore are important to you.

SAPPING AND ZAPPING

> *Never spend time with people
> who don't respect you.*
>
> *- Maori proverb*

We can't always eliminate spending time with people. You may have

a supervisor or a parent whom you don't want to talk to. However, you

can limit the amount of time you spend with such persons or put time

restrictions on people who seemingly want to dominate your time.

Another part of this quote alludes to whom you're spending time with in your professional or personal life. Suzanne Bailey once asked in a workshop (1994), "What packs do you travel in?" My question is: "Do you spend time with people who sap you or zap you?" People who sap you drain your energy, time, and enthusiasm. People who zap you energize you, make you feel better, and provide good feedback. To survive in this intense people business, it's essential to spend as much time as possible with people who zap you. If you're a learner, do you spend time with other learners? What learning activities do you participate in?

GRIEVING

Part of this position is grieving – for all that could be and all that is not. The generally accepted stages of grief are denial, anger, bargaining, depression, acceptance. The research indicates that a person tends to move back and forth through these stages. Where are you on a particular issue?

CELEBRATING TRANSITIONS

Building the tightrope while you're walking on it takes a special kind of talent. You need to focus where you're stepping, the resources to make your rope, and the confidence to traverse the void in the neutral

zone. As Williams Bridges writes in *Managing Transitions* (1991),
there are three parts to the change process. There are always the ending,
the neutral zone, and the new beginning. This is true when there is a
change of leadership, a new curriculum, new programs to replace old ones,
any kind of change. The goal is to plan for the change rather than simply
try to weather the storm.

An example would be when a nearby district was changing from the
junior high school organization to the middle school concept. In order to
make sure the community was cognizant of the impending transition,
district officials planned a celebration to mark the end of the long history
of the junior high schools in the community. The planning for the change
with teachers and curriculum had been worked on throughout the year, but
it was extremely important to identify and honor the end of the tradition
with the community as well.

The next year another celebration was planned and held to honor a
new tradition of the middle school programs. The community was well
aware of the change, there had been honoring of the past, and there was a
celebration of a new approach. Planning for change helps people deal with
change.

ACTIVITY 7.3

1. What have been some transitions in your personal or professional life?
2. What ending have you planned?
3. What new beginning have you planned?
4. How have you helped yourself negotiate the neutral zone?

Issue	Ending	Neutral	New Beginning

Where am I in these issues that are bothering me?

MAINTAINING PERSPECTIVE – CORE VALUES

Another perspective is offered by Stephen Covey. What are your

core beliefs? Think of this metaphor: You are wearing a suit coat and

everyone you come in contact with has "post-it" notes. Each request is

a "post-it" note, and those people put it on your suit coat. By the end of

the day, your coat is covered with "post-it" notes. You probably can't

remember everything because the winds of change come along during the

day and blow the "post-it" notes off your coat. The ones that stick are the ones that touch your core. Covey calls it "true north." So … what are

your beliefs, values, and guiding principles of leadership? What will you

do, and what will you not do? It is these values that will guide you during

turmoil.

ACTIVITY 7.4

Which "post-it" notes
are on your coat right
now?

BECOME YOUR OWN COACH

~ By reading outside your discipline.

~ By developing a new hobby or interest.

~ By developing a small cadre of friends with whom you can
   discuss "on the edge" issues.

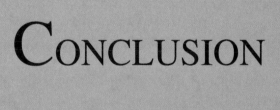

CONCLUSION

C onclusion

In conclusion, the ability to walk the tightrope is the current definition of the principalship. It is not just enough to stay on it; a person has to be able to be moving in a direction as well.

The understanding of and ability to create infrastructure are crucial. The emotional stamina that comes from dealing with crisis after crisis forges identity and skills. Increasingly, the need to resolve both group and individual conflicts defines the day-to-day reality of the principalship.

Joe Jaworski, in his book *Synchronicity*, makes this statement: "If individuals and organizations operate from the generative orientation, from possibility rather than resignation, we can create the future into which we are living, as opposed to merely reacting to it when we get there."

That ability to create the future, as opposed to merely reacting to it, defines the successful principal.

APPENDIX

CAMPUSWIDE INTERVENTIONS THAT
IMPROVE STUDENT ACHIEVEMENT

by Ruby K. Payne, Ph.D.
Educational Consultant

'With simpler models of staff development that are operational and involve 100% of the staff, the roller-coaster ride that students take through school can be smoothed out significantly.'

Conversation between a principal new to the building and a supervisor:
Supervisor: "This campus cannot be low-performing again. I do not have any extra money to give you. With the Title I money you have at your campus, your school will need to find a way to raise your achievement significantly."
Principal (to herself as she walks to the car): "And just how is this to happen? I have 1,100 students, 80% low-income, 12 new teachers, a mobility rate of 40%. I know it can be done, but in a year?"

Many of our models for staff development and curriculum development do not address realities pressuring schools today. Some of these realities are:

~ The critical mass needed to impact student achievement. Example: Ninety percent of teachers are not doing a particular intervention or strategy versus 10% doing it.
~ The growing knowledge base required of teachers and administrators. Example: Educators are to know about sexual harassment, inclusion, cooperative learning, reading strategies, ADHD, modifications, gifted/talented strategies, legal guidelines, ESL strategies, etc.
~ The time frames in which student achievement is to occur and be measured. Example: State and norm-referenced tests are designed for annual measures of learning.
~ The accountability criteria that schools must meet. Example: In Texas, Academic Excellence Indicator System data and Texas Assessment of Academic Skills data are used to determine accreditation status.
~ The lack of money and time for extensive training for teachers. Example: Most districts and campuses have five days or less of staff development, which limits the length and/or depth of the training.
~ The increased number of students who come from poverty and/or who lack support systems at home. Example: When the school system does not address their children's needs, educated parents tend to provide assistance, pay for a tutor, or request a teacher. In poverty, usually the only interventions a student receives are through school.
~ The growing number of new teachers spurred by the surge in the school-age population. Example: The school-age population in America is expected to increase 25% by 2010.

Processes and models are available to address these needs. But to do so, an additional model for staff development and curriculum development must be used. This model basically trades in-depth learning for critical mass by using a simpler approach. Michael Fullan talks about the importance of critical mass, as well as the main criteria teachers use to determine how "user friendly" the curriculum and training are, i.e., how operational they are (Fullan, 1991; Fullan, 1996).

In these models, which I have used for several years, the amount of time spent in training is decreased, the model is less complex and totally operational, and 100% of the staff is trained. We still will need reflective staff development; we just need an additional model to help address some of the aforementioned issues.

Figure A

Factors Affecting Staff Development	Reflective Staff Development	Operational Staff Development
Definition	Process by which individual examines in-depth his/her learning on given subject	Method for immediate implementation across system to address accountability and student achievement
Purpose	To build in-depth learning and change	To impact system quickly; to build in connections/linkages across system
Effect on critical mass	Depends on amount of resources and level of attrition; takes at least four to five years	Affects critical mass almost immediately; can have 80% to 90% implementation first year
Time required	Four to five days per person for initial training	Two hours to one day of training per person
Breadth	Limited	Systemic
Cost analysis	High per-person cost	Low per-person cost
District role	May be contracted or may use district expertise to deliver and provide follow-up	Identifies with campuses' systemic needs to be addressed; works with campuses to reach critical mass; assists with operational development of innovation
Follow-up	Provided in small groups or by expert trainer	Provided through accountability measures and fine-tuning from discussions to make innovation more user-friendly
Role of principal	Is liaison with training; may provide resources and follow-up opportunities	Assists with delivery of training; provides insistence, expectations, and support for innovation

What does this information mean in practice? With simpler models that are operational and involve 100% of the staff, the roller-coaster ride that students take through school can be smoothed out significantly. One of the reasons that most middle-class students do better in school is that their parents intervene to lessen the impact of the roller coaster. (These parents do so by paying for tutoring, requesting teachers, and providing assistance and instruction at home.)

Figure B

Johnny's Progress	Grade 1	Grade 2	Grade 3	Grade 4	Grade 5
Grade 1	X				
Grade 2	X				
Grade 3		X			
Grade 4		X			
Grade 5					

As you can see in Figure B, the X represents Johnny and his journey through five years of school. In first grade, he had a wonderful teacher who willingly went to every kind of training available. Johnny had a great year and made the expected progress.

In second grade, his teacher was having many health problems and missed quite a few days of school. In addition, Johnny's parents divorced, so he was shuttled between homes. In second grade, Johnny actually regressed.

In third grade, Johnny had a beginning teacher. She loved the students but did not have the experience or the guidelines to provide the instruction the other third-grade teacher did. Most of the educated parents had asked for the other teacher because of her excellent reputation. Johnny made little progress.

In fourth grade, Johnny had a teacher who did not participate in staff development. As far as she was concerned, it was a waste of time. Her students tended to do poorly on the state test, but her husband was on the school board. Once again, given her reputation, the educated parents had requested that their children be placed in the other fourth-grade classroom.

In fifth grade, it was determined that Johnny was now 2½ grade levels behind and should possibly be tested for Special Education.

How can we address this problem? With systemic interventions that can impact achievement through simple yet effective tools and processes.

Benjamin Bloom (1976) did extensive research to determine what makes a difference in learning. He identified four factors: (1) the amount of time to learn, (2) the intervention(s) of the teacher, (3) how clear the focus of the instruction is, and (4) what the student came in knowing. As is readily apparent, the control the individual teacher has over these variables is significantly impacted by what is happening at the school. When these interventions are addressed on a campuswide level in a systematic way, more learning occurs.

Systemic interventions that can impact achievement are:

1. *Reasonable expectations.* This is a simple model of curriculum mapping that addresses the focus of instruction and the amount of time.
2. *Growth assessments.* These are methods for identifying and assessing on a regular basis the growth a student makes.
3. *Benchmarks.* This is a relatively simple model of three to four indicators by grading period to show whether a student needs an immediate intervention. *It is absolutely crucial for first-grade reading.* Research indicates that a first-grader who isn't in the primer by April of the first-grade year generally doesn't progress beyond the third-grade reading level.
4. *Interventions for the student.* When students are identified through the growth assessments and benchmarks as making inadequate growth, immediate interventions are provided for the student, one of which is allowing more time during the school day.

What follows are a description and example for each of the above. *It is important to note that all of these are working documents of one or two pages so that they can constantly be reassessed.* It is analogous to having a road map: Not all of the details are present. However, the "lay of the land," the choices of route, and the final destination are clear.

Reasonable Expectations

Reasonable expectations identify what is taught and the amount of time devoted to it. This allows a campus to "data mine," i.e., determine the payoff between what actually gets taught, the amount of time given to it, and the corresponding test results. For example, if two hours a day are spent on reading, but only 15 minutes are devoted to students actually reading, the payoff will be less than if 45 minutes of that time are devoted to students actually reading.

Figure C (see next page) is the process used. For each subject area, it requires about 30 to 60 minutes of individual time, one to two hours of grade-level time, and three hours of total faculty time.

Figure D (see pp. 141-142) is an example from Runyan Elementary in Conroe, Texas. The principal is Nancy Harris.

Figure C

One of the first pieces of information that a principal and campus need to know is *what is actually being taught.* Here's a simple process to help find this out:

1. If you are on a six-weeks grading period, divide a paper into six equal pieces. If you are on a nine-weeks grading period, divide a paper into four equal pieces. Have each teacher for each subject area write the units or skills that he/she teaches in each grading period. In other words, what does the teacher usually manage to teach to that grade level in that subject area in that amount of time?

2. Have each grade level meet and discuss one subject area at a time. Do all the teachers at a grade level basically have the same expectations for that grade level in terms of content and skills? Have they come to a consensus about the expectations for that grade level?

3. Have the faculty as a group compare the grade levels 1 through 5, 6 through 8, or 9 through 12. If Johnny was with the school for five years, what would he have the opportunity to learn? What would he not have had the opportunity to learn? Where are the holes in the opportunities to learn?

4. The faculty then uses this information to identify the strengths and weaknesses in the current educational program. Are some things repeated without benefit to achievement? Are some things not ever taught or so lightly brushed over so as not to be of benefit? What is included that could be traded out for something that has a higher payoff in achievement?

5. When the discussion is over, the one-page sheets are revised and given to the appropriate teachers.

6. Twice a year, the principal meets with grade-level teams and, using these sheets, discusses the progress of the learning, adjustments that need to be made, etc. These become working documents and, because of their simplicity, they can easily be revised.

Figure D

Second-Grade Language Arts Curriculum	
(70% fiction, 30% non-fiction)	
First six weeks	**Second six weeks**
Reading – 60 minutes DEAR (Drop Everything and Read) – 10 minutes Teacher reading to students Reading workshop – 50 minutes	*Reading – 60 minutes* DEAR – 10 minutes Teacher reading to students Reading workshop – 50 minutes
Spelling – 15 minutes, 60 words total 10 *words/week*	*Spelling – 15 minutes, 60 words total* 10 *words/week*

Writing – 45 minutes
Personal narrative, two to three sentences,
    same subject
DOL (Daily Oral Language) – 15 minutes
Writing workshop – 30 minutes
	Writing – 45 minutes
	Six to seven lines on same subject
	    for how-to
	DOL – 15 minutes
	Writing workshop – 30 minutes

Vocabulary (integrated) – five words/week	*Vocabulary (integrated) – five words/week*
Skills – 20 minutes Choosing a just-right book Characters Predicting Distinguishing between fiction and non-fiction	*Skills – 20 minutes* Setting Beginning, middle, end of story Parts of speech: noun, verb Sequential order Comprehension Compound words Contractions

Third six weeks	**Fourth six weeks**
Reading – 60 minutes DEAR – 10 minutes Teacher reading to students Reading workshop – 50 minutes	*Reading – 60 minutes* DEAR – 15 minutes Teacher reading to students Reading workshop – 45 minutes
Spelling – 15 minutes, 60 words total 10 *words/week*	*Spelling – 15 minutes, 60 words total* 10 *words/week* ABC order to second letter

Writing – 45 minutes
Five to seven steps in paragraph form,
    sequential for how-to
DOL – 15 minutes
	Writing – 45 minutes
	How-to: five to seven steps in paragraph form
	DOL – 15 minutes, TAAS (Texas Assessment
	    of Academic Skills) form

Third six weeks (continued)	**Fourth six weeks** (continued)
Writing workshop – 30 minutes *Vocabulary (integrated) – five words/week* *Skills – 20 minutes* Main idea Prefixes, suffixes Context clues Synonyms, antonyms, homophones, homonyms Comprehension Compound words Contractions	Writing workshop – 30 minutes *Vocabulary (integrated) – five words/week* *Skills – 20 minutes* Quotes Draw conclusions Make inferences Adjectives/adverbs Comprehension Possessives Compound words Contractions

Fifth six weeks	**Sixth six weeks**
Reading – 60 minutes DEAR – 15 minutes Teacher reading to students Reading workshop – 45 minutes *Spelling – 15 minutes, 60 words total* 10 *words/week* ABC order to second letter *Writing – 45 minutes* Descriptive writing – seven sentences Compare/contrast DOL – 15 minutes, TAAS form Writing workshop – 30 minutes *Vocabulary (integrated) – five words/ week* *Skills – 20 minutes* Main idea distinguished from details Fact/opinion Cause/effect Comprehension Possessives Compound words Contractions	*Reading – 60 minutes* DEAR – 15 minutes Teacher reading to students Reading workshop – 45 minutes *Spelling – 15 minutes, 60 words total* 10 *words/week* ABC order to third letter *Writing – 45 minutes* Summary Compare/contrast DOL – 15 minutes, TAAS form Writing workshop – 30 minutes *Vocabulary (integrated) – five words/week* *Skills – 20 minutes* Recognize propaganda and point of view Comprehension Possessives Compound words Contractions

Growth Assessments

Any number of growth assessments are available. What makes something a growth assessment is that it identifies movement against a constant set of criteria. What makes a growth assessment different from a test is that the criteria do not change in a growth assessment. Rubrics are one way to measure and identify growth.

Figure E (see next page) is an example of a reading rubric to measure student growth. It was developed by Sandra Duree, Karen Coffey, and me in conjunction with the teachers of Goose Creek Consolidated Independent School District, Baytown, Texas. *Becoming a Nation of Readers* identifies characteristics of skilled readers, so those characteristics were used to measure growth as a constant over five years. We identify what growth would look like over five years if a student were progressing as a skilled reader.

To develop a growth assessment, a very simple process can be used. Have the teachers in your building (who consistently get the highest achievement and who understand the district curriculum and statewide educational specs) develop the growth assessment. Keep in mind these guidelines: (1) The purpose is to identify the desired level of achievement, (2) the growth assessment needs to be simple and easily understood, and (3) student movement or growth toward the desired level of achievement must be clear.

Here are the steps for creating a growth assessment:

1. Identify three to five criteria.
2. Set up a grid with numerical values (1 through 4 is usually enough).
3. Identify what would be an excellent piece of work or demonstration. That becomes #4.
4. Work backwards: Next identify what would be a 3 and so on.

When the growth assessment is developed, it needs to go back to the faculty for feedback and refinement. When there is substantial agreement and at least 80% buy-in, the faculty needs to move forward with it.

Figure E

Reading Rubric, Grade 1			

Student name: _____ School year: _____
Campus: _____ Grade: _____

	Beginning	**Developing**	**Capable**	**Expert**
Fluency	Decodes words haltingly	Decodes sentences haltingly	Knows vowel teams (ea, ee, oa, etc.)	Decodes polysyllabic words
	Misses key sounds	Knows conditions for long vowels (vowel at end of syllable, e.g., me, he)	Identifies common spelling patterns	Decodes words in context of paragraphs
	Identifies most letter sounds	Identifies blends and consonants	Uses word-attack skills to identify new words	Decodes words accurately and automatically
	Identifies short vowels	Decodes diagraphs and r-control vowels (or, ar, er, etc.)	Reads sentences in meaningful sequence	Reads paragraphs in meaningful sequence
	Says/recognizes individual words	Reads at rate that doesn't interfere with meaning	Reads with expression	Reads with expression, fluency, appropriate tone, and pronunciation
Constructive	Predictions are incomplete, partial, and unrelated	Predicts what might happen next	Predicts story based upon pictures and other clues	Can predict possible endings to story with some accuracy
	Predictions indicate no or inappropriate prior knowledge	Makes minimal links to personal experience/prior knowledge	Relates story to personal experience/prior knowledge	Can compare/contrast story with personal experience
Motivated	Does not read independently	Reads when teacher or parent requests	Will read for specific purpose	Initiates reading on own
	Concentrates on decoding	Is eager to use acquired skills (words and phrases)	Uses new skills frequently in self-selected reading	Reads for pleasure

Figure E (continued)

Strategic	Does not self-correct	Recognizes mistakes but has difficulty in self-correcting	Has strategies for self-correction (reread, read ahead, ask questions, etc.)	Analyzes self-correction strategies as to best strategy
	Is uncertain as to how parts of story fit together	Can identify characters and setting in story	Can identify characters, setting, and events of story	Can talk about story in terms of problem and/or goal
Process	Cannot tell what has been read	Does not sort important from unimportant	Can determine with assistance what is important and unimportant	Organizes reading by sorting important from unimportant

Benchmarks

Figure F (see next page) is one example. As you can see from the example, benchmarks are very simple. They identify the critical attributes that students must acquire each six weeks if they are to progress. If the student has not demonstrated these benchmarks, then immediate additional interventions must begin.

How does one get benchmarks? Once again, identify the experienced educators who always have high student achievement. Ask them how they know a student will have trouble. They already know the criteria. And by putting it in writing and having a common understanding, teachers, particularly those who are new to teaching or who are not as experienced, can more readily make interventions and address student progress. It then needs to go back to the grade level for their feedback and changes.

Figure F

Benchmarks for Fourth-grade Language Arts

If a student cannot do the following, then immediate interventions need to be made.

First six weeks
- Edit fragments and run-ons in own writing.
- Identify and define figurative and literal meaning.
- Write elaborated, organized descriptive paper.
- Be able to choose just-right books.

Second six weeks
- Identify story structure orally and in written form.
- Write organized, elaborated expressive narrative.
- Identify correct subject/verb agreement and use in everyday writing.
- Use correct pronoun forms in everyday writing.

Third six weeks
- Read passage and use contextual clues to decode unknown words.
- Read passage and recall facts and details orally and in writing.
- Read story or paragraph and sequence major events.
- Write organized, elaborated how-to.

Fourth six weeks
- Read passage and identify main idea, orally and in written summary.
- Read passage and paraphrase orally and in writing.
- Write organized, elaborated classificatory paper.
- Read passage and identify best summary.
- Write three- to four-sentence paragraph.

Fifth six weeks
- Use graphic sources to answer questions.
- Read passage, then predict outcomes and draw conclusions.
- Distinguish between fact and non-fact, between stated and non-stated opinion.
- After reading passage, be able to tell cause of event or effect of action.
- Write organized, elaborated persuasive paper.

Sixth six weeks
- Write assessment of chosen portfolio pieces.
- Assemble/share reading/writing portfolio.

Interventions for the Student

The issue here is that the intervention be timely and occur at a classroom and a campus level. One other point is simply that for optimal learning, the student needs to stay with the regular instruction, inasmuch as possible, to have the opportunity to learn what the other students are learning. Additional time for learning must be found (e.g., using social studies time to teach non-fiction reading).

Hidden Rules

A final point is that as we work with students from all socioeconomic groups it's important to understand the hidden rules that shape how people think and who people are. The grid below gives an overview of some of the key hidden rules among the classes of poverty, middle class and wealth.

Figure G

Hidden Rules Among Classes			
	Poverty	**Middle Class**	**Wealth**
Possessions	People.	Things.	One-of-a-kind objects, legacies, pedigrees.
Money	To be used, spent.	To be managed.	To be conserved, invested.
Personality	Is for entertainment. Sense of humor is highly valued.	Is for acquisition and stability. Achievement is highly valued.	Is for connections. Financial, political, social connections are highly valued.
Social emphasis	Social inclusion of people he/she likes.	Emphasis is on self-governance and self-sufficiency.	Emphasis is on social exclusion.
Food	Key question: Did you have enough? Quantity important.	Key question: Did you like it? Quality important.	Key question: Was it presented well? Presentation important.
Clothing	Clothing valued for individual style and expression of personality.	Clothing valued for its quality and acceptance into norm of middle class. Label important.	Clothing valued for its artistic sense and expression. Designer important.
Time	Present most important. Decisions made for moment based on feelings or survival.	Future most important. Decisions made against future ramifications.	Traditions and history most important. Decisions made partially on basis of tradition and decorum.
Education	Valued and revered as abstract but not as reality.	Crucial for climbing success ladder and making money.	Necessary tradition for making and maintaining connections.
Destiny	Believes in fate. Cannot do much to mitigate chance.	Believes in choice. Can change future with good choices now.	Noblesse oblige.
Language	Casual register. Language is about survival.	Formal register. Language is about negotiation.	Formal register. Language is about networking.
Family structure	Tends to be matriarchal.	Tends to be patriarchal.	Depends on who has money.
World view	Sees world in terms of local setting.	Sees world in terms of national setting.	Sees world in terms of international view.
Love	Love and acceptance conditional, based upon whether individual is liked.	Love and acceptance conditional and based largely upon achievement.	Love and acceptance conditional and related to social standing and connections.
Driving force	Survival, relationships, entertainment	Work, achievement.	Financial, political, social connections
Humor	About people and sex	About situations.	About social faux pas.

Conclusion

What these systemic interventions allow a campus to do is to address Bloom's four variables in learning: (1) the amount of time to learn, (2) the intervention(s) of the teacher, (3) how clear the focus of the instruction is, and (4) what the student came in knowing.

This approach allows the faculty to address the amount of time, the interventions, the clarity of the instructional focus, and what the student had the opportunity to come in knowing. Right now, because of the depth and breadth of most curriculum guides, it is difficult to know what the students actually had the opportunity to learn. By having these systemic items in place, the faculty discussion can truly be data-driven; it allows the faculty to talk about student achievement in relationship to the total curriculum.

The discussion can focus on program strengths and weaknesses. It can identify areas where more time needs to be devoted and can address the effectiveness of both the whole and the component parts of the curriculum. It allows a faculty to determine staff development that will address student needs, and it provides one more tool for analyzing statewide educational data. Currently, many campuses address the test objective they were low in the year before, only to fall in other objectives the next year. This system allows a new teacher to have a much better sense of expectations. Parents also have a much better sense of the learning opportunities their children will have. It provides a tool for principals and teachers to dialogue about learning. But more importantly, it allows the campus to identify, before the damage is great, the students who aren't making sufficient progress – and to make that intervention immediately, as opposed to one or two years down the road.

This is the process I used as a principal. Our math scores made significant improvement within two years. I have used it at the secondary level in language arts with excellent results as well.

These simple models and processes give us the tools to talk about what we are doing and to minimize the unnerving roller-coaster ride for students.

References

Becoming a Nation of Readers. (1984). Center for the Study of Reading. Champaign, IL: University of Illinois.

Bloom, Benjamin. (1976). *Human Characteristics and School Learning.* New York, NY: McGraw Hill.

Fullan, Michael G. (1991). Turning systemic thinking on its head. *Phi Delta Kappan.* February. pp. 420-423.

Fullan, Michael G. (1996). *The New Meaning of Educational Change.* New York, NY: Teachers College Press, Columbia University.

ANNOTATED

BIBLIOGRAPHY

CHAPTER ONE: ANCHOR OF STRATEGIC ARCHITECTURE

NOTE: In this Annotated Bibliography author Sommers summarizes and reflects on a number of helpful resources for principals.

Ackoff, Russell L. (1991). *Ackoff's Fables.* New York, NY: John Wiley & Sons.

It is my contention that most systems created to promote development actually prevent or retard it. We must learn how to beat these obstructive systems. The system referred to in this expression is generally a bureaucracy. Beating the system has become essential for those who want to develop as rapidly as possible. There is no educational system – most of which are perfect examples of obstructive bureaucracies – that offers courses on this subject.

Robert Townsend, in *Up the Organization*, reports that the British created a civil-service job in 1803 calling for a sentry to stand on the cliffs of Dover. The man was supposed to ring a bell if he saw Napoleon coming. The job was abolished in 1945.

Bureaucracy obstructs development. Although education requires learning, learning does not require teaching. The educational system has demonstrated an unlimited ability to resist responding to its problems. The preoccupation of educators with what students need to know can only be justified if the educators know:

1. What the students are going to do after graduation.
2. What they are going to need to know to do it well.

Educators know neither.

Outside of school, problems are seldom "given"; they usually have to be taken, extracted from complex situations. For the most part, students are not taught how to do this. They are seldom even made aware of the need to do it.

Barth, Roland S. (1990). *Improving Schools from Within.* San Francisco, CA: Jossey-Bass Publishers.

The most crucial role of the principal is as head learner.

A key to improving schools within, then, lies in improving the interactions among teachers and between teachers and principals.

Barth: "School Improvement Team does not make either for a team or for school improvement. It makes for three teachers, two parents, a principal, and a student sitting around a table. The task is not easy. School people working together can assist conditions to make improvements."

Central to my conception of a good school and a healthy workplace is community. In a community of learners, adults and children learn simultaneously to think critically and analytically and to solve problems that are important to them. In a community of learners, learning is endemic and mutually visible.

Block, Peter. (1993). *Stewardship – Choosing Service Over Self-Interest.* San Francisco, CA: Berrett-Koehler Publishers.

Success in the future will depend on organizations that can create new knowledge that results in innovative products and services in the marketplace. Strategies of control and consistency tend to be expensive, are slow to react to the marketplace, and drain passion from human beings.

Besides not being conducive to learning, performance appraisals as we know them are a mistake from the viewpoint of accountability. We should be evaluated by those to whom we are accountable. Stewardship means accountability to those over whom we have power. If you insist on having an appraisal process, let people be evaluated by their customers.

What truly matters in our lives is measured through conversation. Our dialogue with customers, employees, peers, and our own hearts is the most powerful source of data about where we stand.

Collins, James, & Porras, Jerry. (1994). *Built to Last.* New York, NY: HarperCollins Publishers.

Visionary companies display a remarkable resiliency, an ability to bounce back from adversity. Twelve shared *myths*, followed by the reality:

1. **It takes a great idea to start a great company.** Less likely to have early success.
2. **Visionary companies require great and charismatic visionary leaders.** Clock builders, not time tellers.
3. **The most successful companies exist first and foremost to maximize profits.** Make more money than profit-driven companies.
4. **Visionary companies share a common subset of "correct" core values.** Crucial variable is not ideology but how deeply the company believes its ideology and how consistently the company lives, breathes, and expresses it in all that it does.
5. **The only constant is change.** Core values are rock-solid.
6. **Blue-chip companies play it safe.** Visionary companies focus on "big hairy audacious" goals.
7. **Visionary companies are great places to work – for everyone.** Need to fit with core ideology and demanding standards.
8. **Highly successful companies make their best moves by brilliant and complex strategic planning.** Let's just try a lot of stuff and see what works.
9. **Companies should hire outside CEOs to stimulate fundamental change.** Home-grown by a factor of six.

10. **The most successful companies focus primarily on beating the competition.**
No, they focus on beating themselves.
11. **You can't have your cake and eat it too.** Truly visionary companies reject having to make a choice between stability OR progress. It is AND.
12. **Companies become visionary primarily through "vision statements."** This is only one step in a thousand steps.

Johnson, Susan Moore. (1990). *Teachers at Work.* New York, NY: Basic Books.

TEACHERS ARE BEST SUITED AND POSITIONED TO IMPROVE PUBLIC INSTRUCTION. Sizer: "Teachers are often treated like hired hands. Not surprisingly, they often act like hired hands." The character of the school as a workplace determines not only who teaches, but also how they teach. Sizer again: "In order for the education profession to attract and retain exemplary teachers, schools must become exemplary workplaces."

Supervision – "A worker's autonomy often depends on the way work is supervised." "Independent work is not necessarily interactive." Virtually all teachers from both the public and private sectors agreed that, if they are to learn and grow in their work, supervision for improved performance should be separated from evaluation decisions that determine salary or job status. When teachers feel threatened, they conceal their fears and their weaknesses, treating classroom observations as occasions for parading their strengths and teaching surefire lessons rather than venturing forth.

We found no evidence that good teachers profit from the process as it currently stands, with its emphasis on procedural correctness and minimal standards. Two changes seem appropriate. The first would disengage supervision from evaluation, so those who would use the opportunity to explore new approaches could do so unencumbered by the caution that formal evaluation engenders. Teachers judged to be in need of remedial work could participate in a separate process. Second, teachers should be granted, and should assume, greater responsibility for supervising their peers.

Policymakers should abandon industrial models of schooling that prize standardization or promote narrow measures of productivity; they must redirect their attention to improving teaching and learning for the sake of inquiry and higher-order thinking. If public education is to retain its best teachers – those who are creative and skilled, who think for themselves and devise alternative approaches to old problems – then districts should not presume to specify how teachers should do their work or assess their progress narrowly. If we expect children to learn to think, create, and develop their strengths, they must have teachers who are free to do so as well!

According to Johnson's research, effective principals were those who made good teaching possible.

Kidder, Tracy. (1981). *Soul of a New Machine.* New York, NY: Avon Books.

As a leader, I try not to push others any harder than I would push myself – that is how you sign people up. You never con them. Build teams that:

1. Work hard and play well.
2. Don't work for money.

What do you want in people? Look for a passion and a goal, NOT content. Trust is risk, business is risk avoidance. Some problems are easy to find, hard to fix. Being a risktaker in organizations is like playing pinball used to be – YOU WIN ONE GAME, YOU GET TO PLAY ANOTHER.

Land, George, & Jarman, Beth. (1992). *Break-Point and Beyond.* New York, NY: HarperBusiness.

Modification of our thinking patterns will not work. This new era requires a radical rethinking of the most basic and foundational ways we view the world.

The authors suggest three steps in getting to a new organization. First is creativity. Creativity and adaptability are a natural process. Second is connectedness. Everything is connected, and that is why we need to think systemically rather than simply in problem and solution, which usually spin off unintended consequences. Third is future pull. It is increasingly important to think about what is the future pulling us toward. This requires time and thought.

The authors also describe traps that keep organizations from moving to adapt to change. The speed and kind of change are shifting, so they recommend we start understanding the process of change since it will dictate how organizations need to be structured and how leaders will need to manage people.

Miller, Lawrence M. (1989). *Barbarians to Bureaucrats.* New York, NY: Fawcett.

The author describes the normal process of organizations. If the leader does not intercede and plan for the normal cycle, this process will die out and have to be rejuvenated, which is harder to do.

During growth, leaders respond creatively to challenge. During decline, they respond mechanically, relying on responses that have been successful in the past.

The failure of leadership in the corporation is often a consequence of a failure to understand the relationship between the internal strength of the society and the ability to exert external influence.

If there is one lesson in this book, let it be that the decline in corporate culture precedes – and is the primary causal factor in – the decline of a business, and that decline is the result of the behavior and spirit of its leaders.

Five stages and five leadership styles are important to recognize:

1. The Prophet – the visionary who creates the breakthrough and the human energy to propel the school forward.
2. The Barbarian – the leader of crisis and conquest who commands the enterprise on the march of rapid growth.
3. The Manager – the creator of the integrating system and structure, who shifts the focus from expansion to security.
4. The Bureaucrat – the imposer of a tight grip of control, who crucifies and exiles new Prophets and Barbarians, ensuring the loss of creativity and expansion.
5. The Aristocrat – the inheritor of a well-performing system, alienated from those who do productive work, who is the cause of rebellion and disintegration.

Left to go through all the above stages, the system requires a Synergist – the leader who maintains the balance, who continues the forward motion of a large and complex structure by unifying and appreciating the diverse contribution of the Prophet, Barbarian, and Manager.

Rosenholtz, Susan J. (1989). *Teachers' Workplace.* New York, NY: Longman.

This study relies on four measures of organizational effectiveness:

1. School problem-solving and renewal capabilities – or teachers' opportunity to learn.
2. Satisfaction of individual needs – or teachers' certainty about instructional practice.
3. Maintaining motivation and values – or teachers' workplace commitment.
4. School productivity – or measuring student learning outcomes.

Principals are the indisputable linchpin in helping poorly performing teachers to improve. When asked directly about district goals, the superintendent in Richland Hills, Texas, said, "To get better every year in helping teachers teach."

In selecting principals: Superintendents make it clear through their actions that, above all else, principals must be continuous learners and, through their leadership, entice teachers to be learners, too. Four thousand American personnel directors from the private sector ranked non-academic traits and skills substantially higher than academic performance as factors important to workplace success (Crain, 1984; Bills, 1988).

We find that the greater the teachers' opportunities for learning, the more their students tend to learn. The greater the opportunities for teachers to learn, the higher is their students' reading performance. And teachers' learning opportunities monolithically predict math achievement; the greater the teacher opportunity for learning, the greater the students' learning of basic math skills.

One of Rosenholtz's conclusions is that teacher efficacy affects student learning gains and helps build positive relationships. For these findings she cited research by Ashton and Webb (1986), Gibson and Dembo (1979), Berman and McLaughlin (1977).

Teachers can have verifiable effects on student achievement. An immense value is in reflective teaching. In HIGH-consensus schools there is a belief that teachers affect student learning and thus teaching is important. This is marked by a spirit of continuous improvement in which no teacher ever stops learning how to teach.

Study: Samson, Grave, Weinstein, and Walberg (1984) conclude that measures of students' academic achievement, such as grade-point average and scores on conventional standardized tests, accounted for less than 3% of the difference found in such occupational performance measures as income, job satisfaction, and work effectiveness.

Schein, Edgar. (1992). *Organizational Culture and Leadership.* San Francisco, CA: Jossey-Bass Publishers.

The challenge lies in conceptualizing a culture of innovation in which learning, adaptation, innovation, and perpetual change are the stable elements. The bottom line for leaders is that if they do not become conscious of the cultures in which they are embedded, those cultures will manage them. Cultural understanding is desirable for all of us, but it is essential to leaders if they are to lead.

If we accept the proposition that the more things change the more they remain the same, it is not because people will it or because of the perversity of the human personality. Rather, it is primarily because of what we think to be "natural." In other words, this proposition is so much a part of us that it's inconceivable that things could be otherwise (Sarason, 1972).

The only way to build a learning culture that continues to learn is for leaders themselves to acknowledge that they do not know and teach others to accept that they do not know. The learning task is then a shared responsibility.

Creativity and innovation are central to learning.

Senge, Peter M. (1990). *The Fifth Discipline.* New York, NY: Doubleday-Currency.

As most have read, the five educational disciplines are: Personal Mastery, Mental Models, Team Learning, Shared Vision, and Systems Thinking. These tenets will become increasingly important as we try to construct learning organizations.

The organizations that will truly excel in the future will be the organizations that discover how to tap people's commitment and capacity to learn at all levels in an organization.

Ray Strata, CEO, Analog Devices: "One of the highest leverage points for improving system performance is the minimization of system delays."

Building learning organizations involves developing people who learn to see as systems thinkers see, who develop their own personal mastery, and who learn how to surface and restructure mental models collaboratively.

Sergiovanni, Thomas. (1994). *Building Community in Schools.* San Francisco, CA: Jossey-Bass Publishers.

Community building must become the heart of any school improvement effort. How to build community will be a continuing issue, especially since our communities are becoming more diverse.

Stewart, Thomas A. (1997). *Intellectual Capital.* New York, NY: Doubleday-Currency.

"The only irreplaceable capital an organization possesses is the knowledge and ability of its people. The productivity of that capital depends on how effectively people share their competence with those who can use it." - Andrew Carnegie, Industrialist and Philanthropist

This book talks about the need for a new perspective of knowledge as a base for productivity and as a main goal for organizations, including educational institutions. There are three key components: human capital, structural capital, and customer capital.

Intellectual capital is the total knowledge within the company or school. Structural capital is the system set up to deliver that knowledge to the customer. Customer capital is the knowledge your customers have (how does the organization get and use that information to enhance the knowledge, skills, and satisfaction of the organization?).

Stewart calls for new titles and job descriptions in companies. One example is the director of intellectual capital. This job will involve helping the people in the organization keep learning, which is the main competitive advantage.

Human capital and structural capital support each other when the organization has a shared purpose. Human capital and customer capital increase when individuals feel responsible for their part in the system, interact directly with customers, and know what knowledge and skills customers expect and value. Customer capital and structural capital grow when the company and its customers learn from each other.

Knowledgeable workers need to be managed differently from workers who are in companies now. Suggestions are outlined and guidelines presented for supporting communities of practice.

CHAPTER TWO: SAFETY NET OF RELATIONSHIPS

Bennis, Warren. (1989). *Why Leaders Can't Lead.* San Francisco, CA: Jossey-Bass Publishers.

BENNIS'S FIRST LAW OF ACADEMIC PSEUDODYNAMICS: "Routine work drives out nonroutine work and smothers to death all creative planning, all fundamental change in the university – or any institution."

BENNIS'S SECOND LAW OF ACADEMIC PSEUDODYNAMICS: "Make whatever grand plans you will, but you may be sure the unexpected or the trivial will disturb and disrupt them."

The only capital that really counts is human capital. The leader has at least part of his/her job to assist employees to fulfill their own vision. This is a less altruistic process than you might think.

Chaleff, Ira. (1995). *The Courageous Follower*. San Fancisco, CA: Berrett-Koehler Publishers.

Chaleff offers a different take on leadership and the responsibility of followers to help develop leadership in others (and themselves). The author covers such topics as the loyalty, the power, the value, and the courage of the follower.

Leadership and followership are inextricably linked. The term "followership" in this book does not have negative connotations. Followership is not a synonym for subordinate. There is a symbiotic relationship that exists. Therefore, developing leadership requires developing followership. Just as many famous vocalists were once backup singers, in order to be a leader a person needs to be able to be a follower. We need a dynamic model of followership that balances and supports dynamic leadership.

The five dimensions of courageous followership:

1. The courage to assume responsibility.
2. The courage to serve.
3. The courage to challenge.
4. The courage to participate in transformation.
5. The courage to leave.

We must develop everyone in the organization so the organization can continue to learn and deal with the complexities of the future. Courage is a prerequisite to healthy relationships in systems. Courageous leaders and followers work together, so when circumstances don't let them succeed in the moment they leave, the system enriched by their integrity and commitment, for the next creative endeavor.

De Pree, Max. (1989). *Leadership Is an Art*. New York, NY: Dell Trade.

The art of leadership is liberating people to do what is required of them in the most effective and humane way possible. The leader is the servant of his/her followers in that he/she removes the obstacles that prevent them from doing their jobs. The true leader enables his/her followers to realize their full potential.

De Pree encourages contrary opinions and urges leaders to abandon themselves to the strengths of others. The true leader is a listener. The leader listens to the ideas, needs, aspirations, and wishes of the followers.

Structures have little to do with trust. People build trust.

Perkins, David. (1992). *Smart Schools.* New York, NY: The Free Press.

We want schools to deliver a great deal of knowledge and understanding to a great many students of greatly differing talents with a great range of interests and a great variety of cultural and family backgrounds.

Some say we don't know enough to do a better job. We know enough now to do a much better job of education. The problem comes down to this: We are not putting to work what we know. Students are learning, and teachers are teaching in much the same way they did 20 or 50 years ago. In the age of CDs and VCRs, communications satellites and laptop computers, education remains by and large a traditional craft.

Putting the focus on thoughtfulness in the teaching/learning process is the key to genuine learning that serves students well.

The goal should be toward generative knowledge. We know all too well what we want – everything. Lawrence Cremin, author of *Popular Education and Its Discontents*, says we bedevil education with agendas. We try to solve all our problems by assigning them to educators, not only knowledge but citizenship, moral rectitude, comfortable social relations, a more able work force, etc.

One reason to worry is that the "everything" agenda for schools is an energy vampire. It drains teachers, students, and administrators. Nothing drains energy more than having too many things to do and too little time to do any of them anywhere near well.

Here are three general goals that stick close to the narrower endeavor of education:

- Understanding of knowledge.
- Retention of knowledge.
- Active use of knowledge.

Learning is a consequence of thinking. Understanding, retention, and the active use of knowledge can be brought about only by learning experiences in which learners think about *and think with* what they are learning. As we think about and *with* the content we are learning, we truly learn it.

Walton, Mary. (1986). *The Deming Management Method.* New York, NY: The Putnam Publishing Group.

Management in America (though not all) has moved into what I call retroactive management: focus on the end product. Detached managers apply management by the numbers, management by objectives (MBO).

Everyone doing his/her best is not the answer. Most workers *are* doing their best. It is necessary that people understand the reason for the transformation that is necessary for survival.

The biggest problems are self-inflicted, created right at home by management that is off course in the competitive world today.

Walton, Mary. (1990). *Deming Management at Work.* New York, NY: Perigee.

One of the main causes of economic decline in contemporary times is the prevailing system of management – management by fact: ranking people, plants, teams, divisions, companies, and suppliers with reward and punishment. We have been led astray by faith in adversarial competition.

Perhaps the hardest lesson of all is that there is no such thing as "getting it right" – least of all with the promulgation of quality. Continuous improvement is nothing but the development of ever-better methods.

None of this is hard to understand. None of it is easy to do. Change is threatening. There is no right way. There is no learning without mistakes.

CHAPTER THREE: WINDS OF BELIEF SYSTEMS AND CHANGE

Bridges, William. (1991). *Managing Transitions – Making the Most of Change.* New York, NY: Addison-Wesley Publishing Company.

This book will help you to understand the difficulties you face whenever you try to get people to change the way they do things – the blank stares, muttering, foot-dragging, and subtle sabotage that turn a good plan into an unworkable mess. It also will provide dozens of tactics. The book is organized into four parts:

1. Offers a new and useful perspective on the difficulties ahead.
2. Translates that new understanding into practical actions you can take.
3. Gives you ways to deal with nonstop change, both organizationally and personally.
4. Provides another situation in which to test your new tactics.

Change is the name of the game today, and organizations that can't deal with it effectively aren't likely to be around long. Simple, unquestioning compliance comes along less and less often. Change happens so frequently today that one change isn't complete before another is being launched.

A decade of working with people has convinced me of two things:

1. You simply cannot get the results you need without getting into "that personal stuff." There is no impersonal way to have people stop doing things the old way and start doing things a new way.

2. It doesn't take a degree in psychology to successfully manage people in transition. Transition management takes some abilities you already have, along with some techniques you can easily learn.

Fullan, Michael. (1993). *Changing Forces.* London, England: The Falmer Press.

The future of the world is a learning future. Change is a journey of unknown destination – where problems are our friends, where seeking assistance is a sign of strength, where simultaneous top-down bottom-up initiatives merge, where collegiality and individualism co-exist in productive tension.

What will be needed are the individual as inquirer and learner; mastery and know-how as prime strategies; the leader who expresses but also extends what is valued (enabling others to do the same); teamwork and shared purpose, which accepts both individualism and collectivism as essentials to organizational learning; and the organization that is dynamically connected to its environment, which is necessary to avoid extinction, as environments are always changing.

Teachers' capacities to deal with change, learn from it, and help students learn from it will be vital for the future development of societies.

Alliances and partnerships are major vehicles for learning. Learning consortiums are powerful forces for practitioners and academics to learn from each other while attempting to construct learning organizations together.

Pascale, Richard T. (1990). *Managing on the Edge.* New York, NY: Simon & Schuster.

"The world that we have made as a result of the level of thinking we have done thus far creates problems that we cannot solve at the same level as they were created." - Albert Einstein

Nothing fails like success. Winning organizations are locked in the embrace of a potentially deadly paradox. Their greatest strengths are inevitably the root of weakness. Organizations have a tendency to do what they best know how to do; they are the ultimate conservatives. Couple this with the tendency of dedicated and energetic leadership to drive an organization to be still better at what it already does, and we propel ourselves on a trajectory toward excess. Results may be positive and profitable in the short run, but excesses are fatal over time. Leaders too often fixate on "what is," not on "what might be."

The incremental approach to change is effective when what you want is more of what you've already got. We have grown accustomed to improving things without having to alter the mindset upon which the improvements were predicated, the fundamental truths that no longer warrant questioning and re-examination.

Competitive environments push organizations to their limits; the old mindsets no longer hold. What is disheartening is how slowly we are closing the gap between ourselves and our ever-improving global competitors. While we get better, so do they. A discontinuous improvement in capability is needed, and that entail transformation.

Patterns form a mental infrastructure or mindset. Scientists call it a paradigm. Danger arises when our mental maps cease to fit the territory. The problem with mindsets or paradigms is that we tend to see *through* them, so the degree to which they filter our perception goes unrecognized. The essential activity for keeping our paradigm current is persistent questioning. I will use the term inquiry. Inquiry is the engine of vitality and self-renewal.

A central premise of *Managing on the Edge* is that the task of management is one of creating and breaking paradigms. The trouble is, 99% of managerial attention today is devoted to the techniques that squeeze more out of the existing paradigm, and it's killing us. Tools, techniques, and "how-to" recipes won't do the job without a higher-order, or "hyper," concept of management.

A second task is to suggest explicit checks and balances that provoke inquiry and sustain vitality.

Stacey, Ralph D. (1992). *Managing the Unknowable.* San Francisco, CA: Jossey-Bass Publishers.

This book will be of interest to all managers who would like their organizations to have the creative edge necessary to succeed in the modern world. Constant innovation, not stability, is the key to success in today's business environment. Creative management lies in the reflective pause between a stimulus and the response to it. This book aims to provide "the (reflective) pause that refreshes" for action-driven managers.

Success does not depend on choosing stable equilibrium over explosive instability.

Managers who intuitively understand this third state are not confined to tired old patterns of repetition and imitation.

Success is not stable equilibrium but a dynamic state of bounded instability that is far from equilibrium. Creativity is intimately connected with tension, conflict, and ever-changing perspectives.

CHAPTER FOUR: WALKING THE TIGHTROPE – DEALING WITH CRISIS

Bennis, Warren. (1997). *Managing People Is Like Herding Cats.* Provo, UT: Executive Excellence Publishing.

This applies to being a principal of a building, as well as a university president. During my term as university president, I always felt that presiding over the faculty was like herding cats. Such individualism is part of what makes leading a group of knowledge workers so exciting – and so challenging.

Leaders must respect individual rights, tastes, opinions, and idiosyncrasies. Cats, of course, won't allow themselves to be herded. They may, however, be coaxed, cajoled, persuaded, adored, and gently led. With cats, keep in mind, the dictum is milk before eat. Any leader who dares to think of himself/herself as the "cat's meow" will likely be hissed at and clawed. The recipe calls for more catnip, less catnap.

In classrooms, administrators can't just shout, "Sit down, shut up, and listen." Students expect interaction. Why? Because today people have options and opinions; they have money and mobility; they have education and experience; they have personal computers, modems, faxes, e-mail, CD-ROM, and the Internet. In sum, they have information.

So, to you who aspire to lead people, I say, be humble. Stop trying to "herd cats" and start building trust and mutual respect. Your "cats" will respond. They will sense your purpose, keep your business purring, and even kill your rats.

Alfred North Whitehead: "Every leader, to be effective, must simultaneously adhere to the symbols of change and revision and the symbols of tradition and stability."

What most of us in organizations really want is acceptance, affection, self-esteem. Institutions are more amenable to change when the esteem of all members is preserved and enhanced.

Many institutions are managed well yet very poorly led. The institutional leaders may excel in the ability to handle all the daily routine inputs yet never ask whether the routine should be done in the first place.

Trying to be everything to everyone was diverting me from real leadership. It was burning me out. Power shows the man (or woman). Having power showed me some personal truths. First, it was like "looking for love in all the wrong places."

Anyone in authority is to some extent the hostage of how others perceive him/her. When I had the most power I felt the greatest sense of powerlessness. Another truth: I was never going to be completely happy with positional power, the only kind of power an organization can bestow. What I really wanted was personal power, influence based on voice. As Mary Catherine Bateson puts it, "To compose a life is ongoing."

Bohm, David. (1989). *On Dialogue.* Notes from seminar, Ojai, CA. November 6.

The object of a dialogue is not to analyze things, or to win an argument, or to exchange opinions. Rather, it is to suspend your opinions and look at the opinions – to listen to everybody's opinions, suspend them, and see what all that means.

Costa, Arthur, & Garmston, Robert. (1994). *Cognitive Coaching: a Foundation for Renaissance Schools.* Norwood, MA: Christopher Gordon Press.

Coaching is a process to increase dialogue and authentic communication in our schools. This model that started out as a supervisory process for administrators is now being applied to situations with students, certified and non-certified staff, parents, and the business community.

There are two main goals for this process: first, to become intentional in our behaviors to help us get the desired results we want, which includes developing trust and learning for everyone in our system, and second, to continue to develop people's capacity to generate new options in their problem-solving, increase reflection to reduce error rates, and strengthen relationships that are the building blocks of our organizations.

One way that cognitive coaching does this is through encouraging five states of mind. They are as follows:

1. Efficacy – knowing that I have the capacity to make a difference through my work, and being willing to take the responsibility to do so.
2. Flexibility – knowing that I have and can develop options to consider about my work, and being willing to acknowledge and demonstrate respect and empathy for diverse perspectives.
3. Craftsmanship – knowing that I can continually perfect my craft, and being willing to work toward excellence and pursue ongoing learning.
4. Consciousness – knowing what and how I'm thinking about my work in this moment, and being willing to be aware of my actions and their effects.
5. Interdependence – knowing that we will benefit from my participating in, contributing to, and receiving from professional relationships; and being willing to create and change relationships to benefit our work.

Feuerstein, Reuven. (1988). *Don't Accept Me as I Am.* New York, NY: Plenum Press.

"From all those who taught us – we become enlightened. But from those whom we taught – even more so." - Feuerstein

It is imperative that the educator's belief in the human modifiability be a strong one.

I, for example, am a person who may – and has to – be modified. Full professional development can be obtained only by a longlasting investment of the educator in his/her self-modification. Professional complacency is detrimental to the educational intervention process.

Far too little investment is made in developing learning-to-learn ability.

Attributes:

1. Has a degree of openness.
2. Creates a condition of positive stress.

3. Offers a planned and controlled encounter with tasks that are new.
4. Modifies his/her environment and uses individualized/specialized/customized instruction and mediation.

Fisher, Roger, & Ury, William. (1981). *Getting to YES.* New York, NY: Penguin Books.

The authors offer a mental model to help negotiations. There are three ways to negotiate:

1. Hard – situations are a contest of wills, takes extreme position, holds on.
2. Soft – wants to avoid conflict, makes concessions readily.
3. Principled negotiation – hard on merits, soft on people.

When you bargain over positions, people lock into positions; ego becomes identified with position. Positional bargaining becomes a contest of wills; bitter feelings are generated.

Principled negotiation:

People: Separate the people from the problem.
Interests: Focus on interests, not positions.
Options: Generate a variety of possibilities before deciding what to do.
Criteria: Insist that the result be based on some objective standards.

Glickman, Carl D. (1993). *Renewing America's Schools.* San Francisco, CA: Jossey-Bass Publishers.

In successful schools, faculty members are not treated as subordinates but instead are regarded as the colleagues of administrators and others involved in decisions and actions.
No educational research has ever documented that the best way for students to learn is in a closed classroom with one teacher, yet that arrangement predominates in schools.

Johnson, Barry. (1992). *Polarity Management.* Amherst, MA: HRD Press.

Instead of treating every situation as a problem to solve – as if there's a solution for every issue – start looking at issues as dilemmas, two good points of view or polarities, requiring both mindsets in order to have a healthy organization. Johnson provides a framework to understand polarities and how to manage them so you get the best of both parts.

Because the two sides of a polarity are interdependent, you cannot choose one as a "solution" and neglect the other. The objective of the Polarity Management perspective is to get the best of both opposites while avoiding the limits or extremes of each.

People complain about leaders. When the boss is rigid, they want him/her to be more flexible: "Leaders should listen to reason and be willing to adjust to new circumstances."

When the boss is wishy-washy, workers want the boss to be more clear: "Bosses should let us know what they expect; they should have a clear direction and stick with it."

When the boss reacts, it seldom produces the results he/she desires. One reason these solutions don't work is that we are dealing with polarity, which needs to be managed, but we're treating it as if it were a problem to solve.

Lynch, Dudley, & Kordis, Paul. (1988). *Strategy of the Dolphin.* New York, NY: Fawcett.

This book provides an organizer for the many people and issues we deal with as principals. The graphics and templates alone make this book worth putting on your shelf.

"It's not what happens to you but how you respond to what happens to you that determines the quality of your experience." This well-known adage illustrates why it's important to have a wide repertoire in dealing with and managing conflict. Not everyone will approach you with issues or the same process. The principal's ability to manage is linked to his/her varied repertoire and the flexibility to use it in the moment.

Dolphins realize that one creature's perfect home may have little resemblance to another's. This is an important point.

Abraham Lincoln: "You cannot strengthen the weak by weakening the strong. You cannot build character by taking away man's initiative. You cannot help people permanently by doing for them what they could and should do for themselves."

Ury, William. (1991). *Getting Past NO.* New York, NY: Bantam Books.

This is another practical book to expand the principal's repertoire for responding to issues. The principal's life is becoming more and more improvisation. How well we do depends upon our ability to use the knowledge, skills, and attitudes that we know can help us be successful.

You must face five challenges:

1. Don't react. Control your own behavior. Instead of reacting, you need to regain your mental balance and stay focused on achieving what you want.
2. Disarm your opponent. Help your opponent regain his/her mental balance.
3. Change the game. Stop bargaining over positions and start exploring ways to meet the needs of both sides.

4. Make it easy to say yes.
5. Make it hard to say no.

The breakthrough strategy is counterintuitive: It requires you to do the opposite of what you might naturally do in difficult situations. It is no coincidence that effective negotiators listen far more than they talk.

Paraphrase and ask for corrections. It is not enough for you to listen to your opponent. He/she needs to know that you've heard what he/she has said. So reflect back what you hear. Paraphrasing is one of the most useful techniques in a negotiator's repertoire.

CHAPTER FIVE: CLIMBING THE MOUNTAIN – MOVING YOUR ANCHOR

Gardner, John W. (1963). *Self-Renewal.* New York, NY: Harper & Row Publishers.

All of us in education need to have renewal activities. We cannot only focus on work and the problems that face us. What kind of support system we have may mean the difference between long-term survival and short-term burnout. Gardner wrote about this many years ago.

People who have lost their adaptiveness naturally resist change. The most stubborn protector of his/her own vested interest is the person who has lost the capacity for self-renewal.

1. For self-renewing people, the development of potentialities and the process of self-discovery never ends.
2. The development of abilities is at least in part a dialogue between the individual and the environment.
3. Exploration of the full range of one's own potentialities is not something that the self-renewing person leaves to the whims and vagaries of life.
4. The ultimate goal of the educational system is to shift to the student the burden of pursuing his/her own education.

Nothing is more vital to the renewal of an organization than the system by which able people are nurtured and moved into positions where they can make their contribution.

Wheatley, Margaret J. (1992). *Leadership and the New Science.* San Francisco, CA: Berrett-Koehler Publishers.

We are beginning to recognize organizations as systems, construing them as "learning organizations" and crediting them with some type of self-renewing capacity.

Innovation is fostered by information gathered from new connections; from insights gained by journeys into other disciplines or places; and from active, collegial networks and fluid, open boundaries. Innovation arises from ongoing circles of exchange – where information is not just accumulated or stored but created.

CHAPTER SIX: ANCHOR OF IDENTITY

Bardwick, Judith M. (1986). *The Plateauing Trap.* New York, NY: Bantam Books.

Plateauing is a concept that says when a major aspect of life has stabilized, as it ultimately must, we may feel significantly dissatisfied. Being there is not nearly as satisfying as getting there. Many plateaued people quit working, but stay on the job.

Three kinds of plateauing:

1. Structure – level in the hierarchy
2. Content – what and how you do your job
3. Life – having a personal life

Blanchard, Kenneth, & Peale, Norman Vincent. (1988). *The Power of Ethical Management.* New York, NY: Fawcett.

There is no right way to do a wrong thing. The authors give three guidelines to help make decisions.

Question #1: Is it legal? If the answer is no, there is no need to ask any more questions (legal in terms of civil law, criminal law, company policy, codes of ethics).

Question #2: Is it balanced? Is the decision going to be fair, or will it heavily favor one party over another in the short term or the long term? Lopsided decisions end up lose/lose.

Question #3: How will it make me feel about myself? This focuses on your own emotions and standards of morality. An unethical act will erode self-esteem.

John Wooden: "There is no pillow as soft as a clear conscience."

Catford, Lorna, & Ray, Michael. (1991). *The Path of the Everyday Hero.* Los Angeles, CA: Jeremy Tarcher.

Most people go through stages in their professional and personal life. Authors Catford and Ray provide a template that may be helpful in determining where you and your staff are on your respective journeys. Knowing what position people are in provides insights into how to be helpful and supportive.

The individuals who show up every day to work are the everyday heroes and "sheroes."

1. Preparation – Initial stage is having an idea of where you're going or what you want to be.
2. Frustration – Things don't always happen as planned. This becomes a catalyst for your true creativity because it forces you to find an alternative approach and discover your talents and strengths. It is a necessary component of the process.
3. Incubation – Something is percolating, even though you aren't consciously doing anything about it.
4. Strategizing – Most people develop a number of strategies for dealing with their challenges. Those who meet their challenges most creatively and effectively use a range of strategies to invite their creative breakthroughs. They rise to the task like heroes; they don't just sit passively and wait for inspiration to find them.
5. Illumination – This is sometimes referred to as an "Aha!" experience.
6. Verification – Test out an idea and make it real. See how others react to it.

Cooper, Robert, & Sawaf, Ayman. (1997). *Executive EQ*. New York, NY: Grosset/Putnam.

EQ stands for emotional quotient. Modern education and training have been built on a mindset of logic and analysis. A curriculum built on grammar, arithmetic, reductionistic reasoning, formula-driven analyses, and rote memorization of the latest crop of facts is not enough to solve problems in the complex world of education and business. We have tried to be perfect students and by-the-book professionals. Not practical, adaptive, or creative. Not real people but perfect-appearing people, with high IQs and achievements, academically speaking. We've excelled at this model. But it doesn't deal with the most vital things, and it's not enough.

IQ may be related to as little as 4% of real-world success. More than 90% may be related to other forms of intelligence. Relationships are crumbling, trust is vanishing, lawyers are thriving, cynicism is rising, hatred is spreading, and the politics of democracy have been relegated to little more than staged media concoctions. The latest neurological evidence indicates that emotion is the indispensable "fuel" for the brain's higher reasoning powers. Earlier research revealed that, on average, adults use only about 10% of their intelligence in a lifetime. Current brain scientists now believe it may be as little as $1/10,000^{th}$ of one's potential intelligence over a lifetime.

Ninety percent of our believability and credibility may be based on EQ and related practical and creative intelligence – not IQ.

Think about how much time and energy you have wasted protecting yourself from people you don't trust, avoiding problems you cannot talk about, faking acceptance of decisions with which you don't agree, remaining silent despite the intuitive sense that you're missing opportunities, putting up with jobs that aren't right for you, or holding back your insights on current problems and emerging challenges.

Emotions spark creativity, collaboration, initiative, and transformation; logical reasoning reins in errant impulses and aligns purpose with process, technology with touch.

Covey, Stephen R. (1989). *The Seven Habits of Highly Effective People: Powerful Lessons in Personal Change.* New York, NY: Simon & Schuster.

Covey has provided provocative writings for many years regarding leaders' internal guidance systems that help make decisions.

Leadership is a right-brain activity. It's more of an art. Manage from the left, lead from the right. Proactive people focus on their circle of influence. Reactive people focus on their circle of concern.

The seven-habits paradigm:

1. Be Proactive
2. Begin with the End in Mind
3. Put First Things First
4. Think Win/Win
5. Seek First to Understand, Then to Be Understood
6. Synergize
7. Sharpen the Saw

Covey, Stephen R. (1990). *Principle-Centered Leadership.* New York, NY: Simon & Schuster.

In a world where many individuals and groups continually try to advance their agenda, sometimes at the expense of others, the principal must have mental models that provide guidance. This book has been an asset for many leaders for many years.

In school we ask students to tell us what we told them; we test them on our lectures. They figure out the system, party and procrastinate, then cram and feed it back to us to get the grades. Many often think all of life operates on the same short-cut system.

Does cramming work on a farm? Natural laws are the answer; they operate regardless of our awareness of them or our obedience to them. The only thing that endures over time is the law of the farm: I must prepare the ground, put in the seed, cultivate it, weed it, water it, then gradually nurture growth and development to full maturity.

Correct principles are like compasses: They are always pointing the way. If we know how to read them, we won't get lost, confused, or fooled. Principles, unlike values, are objective and external. They operate in obedience to natural laws, regardless of conditions. Values are subjective and internal. Values are like maps. Maps are not the territories, they are merely subjective attempts to describe or represent the territories.

One of the characteristics of authentic leaders is their humility, evident in the ability to take off their glasses and examine the lenses objectively, analyzing how well their values, perceptions, beliefs, and behaviors align with "true north" principles. Centering life on correct principles is the key to developing this rich internal power in our lives. With this power we can realize many of our dreams.

Covey, Stephen R., Merrill, Roger A., & Merrill, Rebecca R. (1994). *First Things First.* New York, NY: Simon & Schuster.

One of the most important decisions principals make is how their time is spent. The quadrants that Covey has provided (see p. 40) suggest one way to determine where and how we should spend our time. Traditional time management suggests that by doing things more efficiently you'll eventually gain control of your life – and that increased control will bring the peace and fulfillment you're looking for. We disagree.

Basing our happiness on our ability to control everything is futile. While we do control our choices of action, we cannot control the consequences of our choices. Universal laws or principles do.

Rather than offering you another clock, this approach provides you with a compass, because more important than how fast you're going is where you're headed.

Frankl, Viktor E. (1959). *Man's Search for Meaning: an Introduction to Logotherapy.* New York, NY: Beacon Press.

This resource has been around for many years. The atrocities of the death camps in Nazi Germany constituted the background of this survivor's writings. Human will can be a major contributor in dealing with difficult situations. The last of the human freedoms is to choose one's attitude in any given set of circumstances, to choose one's own way.

A prisoner who had lost faith in the future, his future, was doomed. With his loss of belief in the future, he also lost his spiritual hold; he let himself decline and became subject to mental and physical decay.

Humor is another of the soul's weapons in the fight for self-preservation. Humor is a trick learned while mastering the art of living.

Garfield, Charles. (1986). *Peak Performers.* New York, NY: Avon Books.

This book surveyed high-performing people in many vocations. Garfield's research wanted to find out what contributes to the best performances in all fields. Peak performers believe, in the final analysis, that they will make it. Peak performance begins with a commitment to a mission. The primary "locus of control" for a peak performer is not external but internal.

Goleman, Daniel. (1995). *Emotional Intelligence.* New York, NY: Bantam Books.

Goleman extended our thinking in how people handle the day-to-day pressures of their position. We can be smart in the traditional academic sense, but principals will have to increase their intelligence in the emotional arena.

New brain research is clear about how this intricate mass of cells operates while we think and feel, imagine and dream. Emotional intelligence includes self-control, zeal, persistence, and the ability to motivate oneself.

The ability to control impulse is the basis of will and character. The root of altruism lies in empathy, the ability to read emotions in others; lacking a sense of another's need or despair, there is no caring. The two moral stances most urgent in our times are self-restraint and compassion.

Perhaps the most disturbing single piece of data in this book comes from a massive survey of parents and teachers that shows a worldwide trend for the present generation of children to be more troubled emotionally than the last: more lonely and depressed, more angry and unruly, more nervous and prone to worry, more impulsive and aggressive.

Our solution is a new vision of what schools can do to educate the whole student. According to Aristotle, the problem is not with emotionality, but with the appropriateness of emotion and its expression. The question is: How can we bring intelligence to our emotions, civility to our streets, and caring to our communal life?

This question will continue to be an issue for everyone involved in education.

Hawley, Jack. (1993). *Reawakening the Spirit in Work: the Power of Dharmic Management.* San Francisco, CA: Berrett-Koehler Publishers.

Our state of mind as principals will impact our efficiency and effectiveness. A lot of literature exists stating the importance of the principal as a main factor in the health of a school building. The principal's modeling will be the philosophy in practice for the rest of the community.

One of the hardest things I have come to realize as a general manager is that my state of mind is really my primary tool. My everyday life is spent dispersing energy; keeping a mental focus at times can feel like a full-time task. Each day I need to redevelop vision and focus.

Energy requires thinking. Thinking requires energy. An organization's energy is managed by changing the intensity and direction of energy. An excellent definition of good management/leadership: arousing and channeling a human system's energy, infusing "oomph."

Kouzes, James M., & Posner, Barry Z. (1993). *Credibility*. San Francisco, CA: Jossey-Bass Publishers.

This book provides some research on leaders and what constituents want from their leaders. A few pieces of their findings are listed below.

The key to unlocking greater leadership potential can be found only when you seek to understand the service relationship. Fifteen hundred managers nationwide provided 225 values, characteristics, and attitudes they consider crucial to leadership. Most frequent responses in order of mention were:

1. Integrity – truthful, trustworthy.
2. Competence – capable, efficient, productive.
3. Leadership – inspiring, decisive, providing direction.

Key characteristics of admired leaders in 1987 and 1993 were:

1. Honest – first step; without honesty there is no chance for leadership.
2. Forward-looking – can see across the horizon of time and imagine what might be.
3. Inspiring – dynamic, enthusiastic, positive, optimistic.
4. Competent – some technical competence and leadership skills.

LaBorde, Genie Z. (1983). *Influencing with Integrity: Management Skills for Communication and Negotiation*. Palo Alto, CA: Syntony Publishing.

Tools that principals use to influence people have long-term effects on the school. This book gives usable skills and resources on how to move from conflict to consensus, as well as personal communication strategies that increase authentic dialogue.

Dovetailing outcomes ensures your own personal integrity and shows respect fort the other person's integrity. Manipulation is the opposite of dovetailing. Dovetailing doubles your chance of getting what you want.

Our reality is affected by three processes that principals need to be aware of in our daily relationships with individuals and groups:

1. Deletion – occurs when we overlook, tune out, or omit.
2. Distortion – a personal prejudice that twists our perceptions.
3. Generalization – when we universalize based on one or two experiences.

Walsh, David. (1994). *Selling Out America's Children*. Minneapolis, MN: Fairview Publishers.

Dr. Walsh provides research about students that all principals should know. The influences in society are strong, and school officials need to know what they can do to influence the future of their students. Walsh also provides guidance for parents, society, and others to positively affect the health of the community's children.

There is growing concern about the effects of excessive competition and consumerism on America's children. There is consensus among parents as to the important values children must learn. I have been struck by the fact that the set of values parents identify is not the one that is supported in our larger society.

The dichotomy between private and societal values has become clearer. My optimism is based on my interactions with so many adults who have not forgotten what values are essential for healthy children. Those values have not been forgotten, but they have become lost in a larger, anonymous society where a different set of values has been promoted – a set that is designed to raise profits, not children.

We will only begin to make progress when we see the whole problem for what it is. Violence grabs the headlines, but violence itself is a result of a society that promotes selfishness, greed, and instant gratification. The first step is to become fully aware of what we are facing.

CHAPTER SEVEN: MAINTAINING YOUR TIGHTROPE –
SELF-RENEWAL

Arrien, Angeles. (1993). *The Four-Fold Way: Walking Paths of the Warrior, Teacher, Healer, and Visionary.* New York, NY: HarperCollins Publishers.

Four tenets are explained in this book. These four have been helpful to me in providing guidance when making decisions that have long-term consequences. They are as follows:

1. Show up and choose to be present.
2. Pay attention to what has heart and meaning.
3. Tell the truth without blame or judgment.
4. Be open to outcome, not attached to outcome.

Autry, James. (1991). *Love and Profit – the Art of Caring Leadership.* New York, NY: Avon Books.

Autry provides five guidelines that help determine how to lead people and how to behave to increase trust and capacity in your staff. They are:

1. Avoid in-box management: sitting at your desk waiting for someone to make a mistake so you'll have something to do.
2. Care about yourself. Charles Garfield: "You don't go through life motivating people; you jump-start them. You can't jump-start anyone unless your own battery is charged."

3. Be honest. Honesty is the single most important attribute in a manager's relationship with employees and fellow workers. Even firing can be an act of caring, though you will rarely be thanked for it.
4. Trust your employees. Most organizations manage to make people feel distrusted.
5. If you don't care about people, get out of management before it's too late. Workers want to know how much you care before they care how much you know.

Merriam, Sharan B. (1993) *An Update on Adult Learning Theory*. San Francisco, CA: Jossey-Bass Publishers.

Self-directedness is viewed as the essence of what adult learning is all about. Adults have felt oppressed by earlier educational experiences and are looking for a way to justify their own responsibility for their own learning.

One of the most powerful motivators for participation in adult learning activities is the need to stay abreast of changes in society that affect one's work and personal life.

As Merriam notes, Howard McCluskey has a Theory of Margin that recognizes that people have less than perfect control over many aspects of life; they must always be prepared to meet unexpected crises or problems.

Margin is the ratio or relationship between "load" (of living) and "power" (to carry the load). Load is "the self and social demands required by a person to maintain a minimal level of autonomy ... Power is the resources, i.e., abilities, possessions, position, allies, etc., which a person can command in coping with load. In other words, $M = L/P$.

The external load consists of tasks involved in normal life requirements (family, work, and community responsibilities).

The internal load consists of life expectancies developed by people (aspirations, desires, and future expectations).

Margin can be increased by reducing load or increasing power. Surplus power is always needed to provide enough margin or cushion to meet various load requirements and life emergencies.

The balancing of demands on life with goals or interests requires the maintenance of some sort of margin.

BIBLIOGRAPHY

Ackoff, Russell L. (1991). *Ackoff's Fables*. New York, NY: John Wiley & Sons.

Amason, Allen, Thompson, Kenneth, Hochwarter, Wayne, and Harrison, Allison. (1995). *Conflict:* an important dimension in successful management teams. New York, NY: Organizational Dynamics. August.

Arrien, Angeles. (1993). *The Four-Fold Way: Walking Paths of the Warrior, Teacher, Healer, and Visionary.* New York, NY: HarperCollins Publishers.

Autry, James. (1991). *Love and Profit – the Art of Caring Leadership.* New York, NY: Avon Books.

Bailey, Suzanne. (1994). Notes from workshop, National Staff Development Council, Chicago, IL. December 8.

Bardwick, Judith M. (1986). *The Plateauing Trap.* New York, NY: Bantam Books.

Barth, Roland S. (1990). *Improving Schools from Within.* San Francisco, CA: Jossey-Bass Publishers.

Beckhard, Richard. (1987). *Organizational Transitions* (2nd Edition). New York, NY: Addison-Wesley Publishing Company.

Bennis, Warren. (1989). *Why Leaders Can't Lead.* San Francisco, CA: Jossey-Bass Publishers.

Bennis, Warren. (1997). *Managing People Is Like Herding Cats.* Provo, UT: Executive Excellence Publishing.

Blanchard, Kenneth, & Peale, Norman Vincent. (1988). *The Power of Ethical Management.* New York, NY: Fawcett.

Block, Peter. (1987). *The Empowered Manager.* San Francisco, CA: Jossey-Bass Publishers.

Block, Peter. (1993). *Stewardship – Choosing Service Over Self-Interest.* San Francisco, CA: Berrett-Koehler Publishers.

Bohm, David. (1989). *On Dialogue.* Notes from seminar, Ojai, CA. November 6.

Bridges, William. (1991). *Managing Transitions – Making the Most of Change.* New York, NY: Addison-Wesley Publishing Company.

Brinkman, Rick, & Kirschner, Rick. (1994). *Dealing with People You Can't Stand.* New York, NY: McGraw Hill.

Brodie, Richard. (1996). *Virus of the Mind.* Seattle, WA: Integral Press.

Catford, Lorna, & Ray, Michael. (1991). *The Path of the Everyday Hero.* Los Angeles, CA: Jeremy Tarcher.

Chadwick, Robert. (1997). *Conflict to Consensus Institute*, Minneapolis, MN. August 16-18.

Chaleff, Ira. (1995). *The Courageous Follower.* San Francisco, CA: Berrett-Koehler Publishers.

Cohen, Herb. (1980). *You Can Negotiate Anything.* New York, NY: Bantam Books.

Collins, James, & Porras, Jerry. (1994). *Built to Last.* New York, NY: HarperCollins Publishers.

Cooper, Robert, & Sawaf, Ayman. (1997). *Executive EQ.* New York, NY: Grosset/Putnam.

Costa, Arthur, & Garmston, Robert. (1994). *Cognitive Coaching: a Foundation for Renaissance Schools.* Norwood, MA: Christopher Gordon Press.

Covey, Stephen R. (1989). *The Seven Habits of Highly Effective People: Powerful Lessons in Personal Change.* New York, NY: Simon & Schuster.

Covey, Stephen R. (1990). *Principle-Centered Leadership.* New York, NY: Simon & Schuster.

Covey, Stephen R., Merrill, Roger A., & Merrill, Rebecca R. (1994). *First Things First.* New York, NY: Simon & Schuster.

Cremin, Lawrence. (1990). *Popular Education and Its Discontents.* New York, NY: Harper & Row Publishers.

Crum, Thomas F. (1987). *The Magic of Conflict.* New York, NY: Touchstone Books, Simon & Schuster.

Csikszentmihalyi, Mihaly. (1990). *FLOW: the Psychology of Optimal Experience.* New York, NY: Harper & Row Publishers.

de Geus, Arie. (1997). *A Living Company*. Cambridge, MA: Harvard Business School Press.

De Pree, Max. (1989). *Leadership Is an Art*. New York, NY: Dell Trade.

Dewey, John. (1933). *How We Think*. Chicago, IL: University of Chicago Press.

Eisner, Elliott, & Vallance, Elizabeth. (1974). *Conflicting Conceptions of Curriculum*. Berkeley, CA: McCutchan Publishing.

Evans, Patricia. (1996). *The Verbally Abusive Relationship*. Holbrook, MA: Adams Media.

Farson, Richard. (1996). *Management of the Absurd*. New York, NY: Touchstone Books.

Ferguson, Marilyn. (1980). *The Aquarian Conspiracy*. Los Angeles, CA: Jeremy Tarcher.

Feuerstein, Reuven. (1988). *Don't Accept Me as I Am*. New York, NY: Plenum Press.

Fisher, Roger, & Ury, William. (1981). *Getting to YES*. New York, NY: Penguin Books.

Forward, Susan. (1997). *Emotional Blackmail*. New York, NY: HarperCollins Publishers.

Frankl, Viktor E. (1959). *Man's Search for Meaning: an Introduction to Logotherapy*. New York, NY: Beacon Press.

Fullan, Michael. (1993). *Changing Forces*. London, England: The Falmer Press.

Gardner, John W. (1963). *Self-Renewal*. New York, NY: Harper & Row Publishers.

Gardner, John W. (1990). *On Leadership*. New York, NY: The Free Press.

Garfield, Charles. (1986). *Peak Performers*. New York, NY: Avon Books.

Gerzon, Mark. (1996). *A House Divided*. New York, NY: Putnam Publishing Co.

Glenn, Stephen. (1985). Notes from workshop, Minnesota Chemical Dependency Association, St. Cloud, MN. November 11.

Glenn, Stephen. (1985). *Developing Capable Young People.* Orem, UT: Empowering People.

Glickman, Carl D. (1993). *Renewing America's Schools.* San Francisco, CA: Jossey-Bass Publishers.

Goleman, Daniel. (1995). *Emotional Intelligence.* New York, NY: Bantam Books.

Gordon, David. (1978). *Therapeutic Metaphors.* Cupertino, CA: Meta Publications.

Greenspan, Stanley. (1997). *The Growth of the Mind and the Endangered Origins of Intelligence.* Reading, MA: Perseus Books.

Grinder, Michael. (1998). *Group Dynamics Training Syllabus.* Battle Ground, WA: Michael Grinder & Associates.

Hawley, Jack. (1993). *Reawakening the Spirit in Work: the Power of Dharmic Management.* San Francisco, CA: Berrett-Koehler Publishers.

Heuerman, Thomas C. (1997). *A More Natural Way: Leadership for Sustainable Organizations.* Unpublished doctoral dissertation.

Johnson, Barry. (1992). *Polarity Management.* Amherst, MA: HRD Press.

Johnson, Susan Moore. (1990). *Teachers at Work.* New York, NY: Basic Books.

Keen, Sam. (1991). *Fire in the Belly.* New York, NY: Bantam Books.

Kidder, Tracy. (1981). *Soul of a New Machine.* New York, NY: Avon Books.

Kohn, Alfie. (1993). *Punished by Rewards.* New York, NY: Houghton Mifflin Company.

Kouzes, James M., & Posner, Barry Z. (1993). *Credibility.* San Francisco, CA: Jossey-Bass Publishers.

LaBorde, Genie Z. (1983). *Influencing with Integrity: Management Skills for Communication and Negotiation.* Palo Alto, CA: Syntony Publishing.

Lambert, Linda, Zimmerman, Diane, et al. (1995). *The Constructivist Leader.* New York, NY: Teachers College Press.

Land, George, & Jarman, Beth. (1992). *Break-Point and Beyond.* New York, NY: HarperBusiness.

Leslau, Charlotte, & Leslau, Wolf. (1962). *African Proverbs*. New York, NY: Peter Pauper Press.

Lynch, Dudley, & Kordis, Paul. (1988). *Strategy of the Dolphin*. New York, NY: Fawcett.

McKenzie, Carole. (1989). *Quotable Women*. Philadelphia, PA: Running Press.

Merriam, Sharan B. (1993). *An Update on Adult Learning Theory*. San Francisco, CA: Jossey-Bass Publishers.

Mikado, Michael. (1991). *Thinkertoys*. Berkeley, CA: Ten Speed Press.

Miller, Lawrence M. (1989). *Barbarians to Bureaucrats*. New York, NY: Fawcett.

Pascale, Richard T. (1990). *Managing on the Edge*. New York, NY: Simon & Schuster.

Pascarella, Perry. (1984). *The New Achievers*. New York, NY: The Free Press.

Payne, Ruby K. (1998). *A Framework for Understanding Poverty* (Revised Edition). Baytown, TX: RFT Publishing Co. (now aha! Process, Inc. of Highlands, TX)

Perkins, David. (1992). *Smart Schools*. New York, NY: The Free Press.

Peters, Tom. (1986). A *Passion for Excellence*. New York, NY: Random House.

Rosenholtz, Susan J. (1989). *Teachers' Workplace*. New York, NY: Longman.

Schein, Edgar. (1992). *Organizational Culture and Leadership*. San Francisco, CA: Jossey-Bass Publishers.

Schwartz, Peter. (1996). *The Art of the Long View*. New York, NY: Doubleday.

Seligman, Martin E.P. (1990). *Learned Optimism*. New York, NY: Alfred A. Knopf.

Senge, Peter M. (1990). *The Fifth Discipline*. New York, NY: Doubleday-Currency.

Sergiovanni, Thomas. (1994). *Building Community in Schools*. San Francisco, CA: Jossey-Bass Publishers.

Sinetar, Marsha. (1991). *Developing a 21st Century Mind*. New York, NY: Villard Books.

Stacey, Ralph D. (1992). *Managing the Unknowable.* San Francisco, CA: Jossey-Bass Publishers.

Stewart, Thomas A. (1997). *Intellectual Capital.* New York, NY: Doubleday-Currency.

Townsend, Robert. (1984). *Up the Organization.* New York, NY: Knopf.

Ury, William. (1991). *Getting Past NO.* New York, NY: Bantam Books.

Walsh, David. (1994). *Selling Out America's Children.* Minneapolis, MN: Fairview Publishers.

Walton, Mary. (1986). *The Deming Management Method.* New York, NY: Perigee.

Walton, Mary. (1990). *Deming Management at Work.* New York, NY: Perigee.

Wheatley, Margaret. (1992). *Leadership and the New Science.* San Francisco, CA: Berrett-Koehler Publishers.

Wheatley, Margaret, & Kellner-Rogers, Myron. (1996). *A Simpler Way.* San Francisco, CA: Berrett-Koehler Publishers.

Whyte, David. (1994). *The Heart Aroused.* New York, NY: Doubleday-Currency.